PATCHWORK
FROM MOSAICS

PATCHWORK FROM MOSAICS

Patchwork from the stones of Venice

Helen Fairfield

with illustrations by the author

Arco Publishing, Inc.
New York

Published 1985 in the United States by
Arco Publishing, Inc.
215 Park Avenue South
New York, N.Y. 10003 ,

Library of Congress Cataloging-in-Publication Data

Fairfield, Helen.
    Patchwork from mosaics.

    Includes index.
    1. Patchwork. 2. Patchwork–Patterns. 3. Mosaics–
Italy.   I. Title.
TT835.F33 1985   746.46   85-9101
ISBN 0-688-06558-3

Printed in Great Britain

Contents

Introduction

When a sudden downpour interrupted our stroll across the Piazza San Marco in Venice, my husband and I took refuge in the Atrium of the Basilica. It was too dark to see clearly the glittering mosaics above us, but the stones at our feet were wet from the rain tracked in by visitors, and glowed with colour. I realized that we were treading upon pattern after pattern of marble patchwork.

The floor of the Basilica is divided into dozens of small areas which were laid independently over a period of about 400 years. The older, pictorial panels are Byzantine in influence, made up of cubes all of the same size, and therefore outside the scope of this book, but the geometric designs laid between the eleventh and the fifteenth centuries could have been designed for working in patchwork. With clever use of shape and shade, the paviors of Venice created intricate designs,

Figure 1

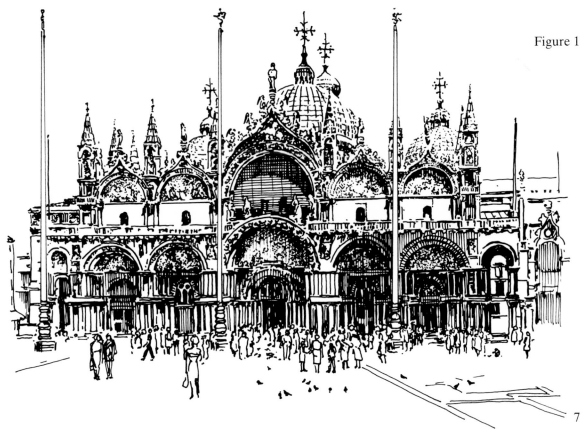

many of which posses remarkable illusions of a third dimension.

It is difficult to understand, let alone explain, why obsessions take hold, but in the remaining three days of our holiday we collected 46 patterns from the floors of St Mark's and other Venetian churches. On our return home, these rough sketches and colour notes were transformed into workable patterns, and I made up a number of them into cushions, hangings and quilts. I tried to keep to the soft colours of the stone, and, as most of the marbles were 'figured', it seemed quite appropriate to use patterned cottons in the manufacture of their fabric replicas.

Realizing that we must have missed a lot, we took the earliest opportunity to return to Venice to make a more systematic 'collection', this time with the additional aid of a camera. You will find the results in the following pages.

A subsequent visit to Florence provided further patterns, some of which were variations of Venetian designs whilst others were quite new. Some of the patterns may look familiar to experienced patchworkers. For instance, the pattern in figure 2, found in San Giorgio Maggiore (built in 1565), is a variation of the American patchwork design known as the Le Moyne Star (figure 3). However, it is very much older than the Venetian floors, as the same pattern, this time in cube mosaic, was uncovered when the Roman Palace at Fishbourne in West Sussex was excavated a few years ago.

Figure 2

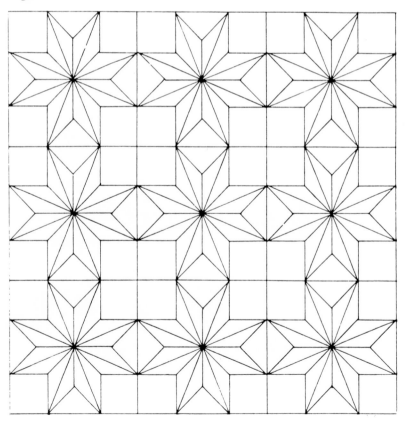

Figure 3

8

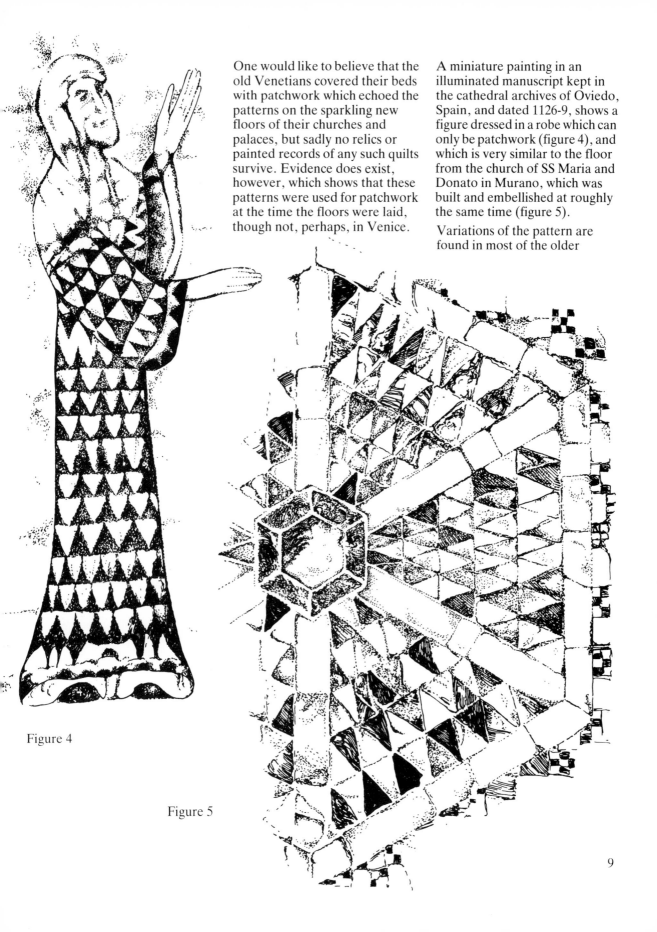

One would like to believe that the old Venetians covered their beds with patchwork which echoed the patterns on the sparkling new floors of their churches and palaces, but sadly no relics or painted records of any such quilts survive. Evidence does exist, however, which shows that these patterns were used for patchwork at the time the floors were laid, though not, perhaps, in Venice.

A miniature painting in an illuminated manuscript kept in the cathedral archives of Oviedo, Spain, and dated 1126-9, shows a figure dressed in a robe which can only be patchwork (figure 4), and which is very similar to the floor from the church of SS Maria and Donato in Murano, which was built and embellished at roughly the same time (figure 5).

Variations of the pattern are found in most of the older

Figure 4

Figure 5

9

Venetian churches and it is one of the commonest designs in St Mark's.

Similarly when, in 1561, J. Annam painted a very busy picture of a tourney at Nuremberg, he dressed a knight's horse and retainer in one of the patterns most frequently found in Venetian churches (figure 6), but commonly known to patchworkers as 'tumbling blocks' or 'baby's blocks' (figure 7).

I hope that the designs we gathered may be of use both to newcomers to patchwork and to those whose knowledge of the craft is wider than mine. I have endeavoured to explain in detail how to make each design into a useful article using 'English' patchwork. Where it is possible or convenient to use the method, I have then translated the design for use in 'American' patchwork. At the end of each chapter, I have included variations we found on the basic design, and designs which seem to fall into the same 'family'.

I hope you will enjoy working those patterns which appeal to you as much as we enjoyed collecting them.

Figure 6

Figure 7

1
Methods

There are two basic methods of joining patchwork pieces together. Traditionally, these are referred to as the 'English' and the 'American' methods, although their respective uses are decided more by the shapes of the designs being attempted than by any nationalistic considerations. Any pieced design can be worked by the English method, but only the most skilled patchworker would attempt some designs the American way, which is best employed where all the main seams can be arranged to run in straight lines across the article.

In the English method, a template is used to mark out the required shapes on to stiff paper. These shapes are cut out carefully and then covered with fabric with ample turnings being stitched on to the back of the paper shapes. The patches thus formed are stitched together by hand, the papers being removed when a patch has been completely surrounded by other patches.

In the American method, the template is used to mark shapes directly onto the wrong side of the fabric with a pencil. The shapes are cut out leaving an adequate

Figure 8

seam allowance all around the shape. Pieces are then stitched together by carefully matching up the pencilled lines, pinning them together, and sewing along these lines by hand or machine.

The beginner will probably find it easier to achieve good results by the English method, and it is suitable for all designs and all shapes of template. The American way is much quicker and, with reasonable care, just as accurate. There are, however, some designs for which the American way is just not suitable unless the templates are considerably modified in order to produce straight lines.

Obviously, the Venetian stonemasons were not governed by our design limitations when they laid their floors. St Mark's has some marvellous combinations of motifs making up 'quilt' designs which could easily be copied in fabric, but which would appear to ask for a combination of the two techniques. Of course, the whole design could be worked in English patchwork, but generally I have found that a minor modification of the design of the templates makes manufacture by the American method quite feasible.

All the designs in this book give instructions for the English method, and, where it can easily be worked, instructions for the American method as well.

The corner of the 'quilt' in figure 8, which we found in the Atrium of St Mark's Basilica, just inside the door from the Piazzetta dei Leoncini, provides a very easy example to start with. In the original version used by the paviors, this pattern could only be translated into English patchwork (figure 9).

HERB CUSHION IN ENGLISH PATCHWORK (see figure 10)

To work the design in the corner of the stone 'quilt' in English patchwork, it is necessary to prepare three templates. These should be drawn out very carefully on squared graph paper and glued to stiff card. When the glue is dry the templates must be cut out very accurately, using a metal ruler and a very sharp knife. Unless the templates are accurate the finished pieces will not fit together.

If each square in the diagram equals 12 mm (½ in.) the patch sizes will be comfortable to work with in English patchwork, and, using the design above, result in a 205 mm (8 in.) square – a useful size for a herb cushion.

Make up three templates (figure 11), measuring and cutting very carefully – a long hexagon, a square, and a triangle formed by cutting the square in half from a to b. Use a very stiff card as your backing. The stiff backing to a sketchbook is ideal.

You will need a supply of stiff paper for your shapes. Used envelopes, cartridge paper, or stiff brown wrapping paper will do. You want a paper stiff enough to hold the shape but not so stiff it is an effort to pierce it with a needle.

For this small sampler you will need to cut four squares, 16

Figure 9

Figure 10

hexagons and eight triangles out of paper (figure 12).

While it is possible to trace these shapes on to the stiff paper and cut them out, your work is likely to be much more accurate if you hold the template against the paper and cut carefully, using paper-cutting scissors, as close as you can to the template (figure 13).

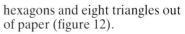

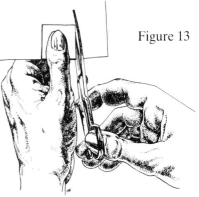

Figure 13

Figure 11

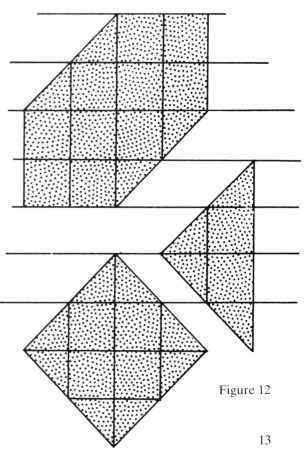

Figure 12

13

To cover your papers you will need four colours of lightweight cotton. The stones of the original floor have squares of a very dark grey marble, the hexagons are figured greys and browns, while the triangles at the edges are a warm, creamy yellow. These colours could be followed in a selection of printed materials, so long as the print patterns are small and not distracting.

Of course, should this colour scheme not appeal to you there is no reason why you should not choose another, so long as you keep the relationship between the tones. For the sake of clarity I shall assume that we are using the original colours of the marble floor.

Pin the four paper squares on to the wrong side of the dark grey material you have chosen, with the edges of the paper shapes parallel to the threads of the fabric. Two pins, parallel with each other, will prevent the fabric from moving when it is being cut and stitched. Make sure you leave ample seam allowances between the shapes and cut out with sharp scissors (figure 14). The seam allowance left around each paper shape should be approximately 6 mm (¼ in.)

Pin eight hexagons on to the wrong side of the light grey material, and eight more on to the wrong side of the light brown cotton, making sure that the long sides of the hexagons lie along the grain of the material. Pin the triangles on to the wrong side of the cream fabric, with the short sides on the straight of the grain. Make sure you have left ample seam allowances. Cut out.

Take each shape in turn, starting with the squares. Thread a sharp needle with tacking cotton, and anchor the thread securely in your work. Methods of fastening are very personal. Some insist that you should start with a backstitch, but I find that the removal of the stitching on completion is made easier if the tacking is started with a knot with a long tail and then finished off with a backstitch.

Fold the extra fabric over to the back of the paper, making sure that while you have the fold flush with the edge of the pattern, the paper is not folded over with the fabric. Stitch it down, and continue around the shape, taking particular care with the corners (figure 15). Finish off with a backstitch and remove the pins.

It is very useful to draw the whole pattern out to size on graph paper and lay it over pinboarding. As each piece is finished, pin it into place on this pattern. Having the pieces pinned into position while

Figure 14

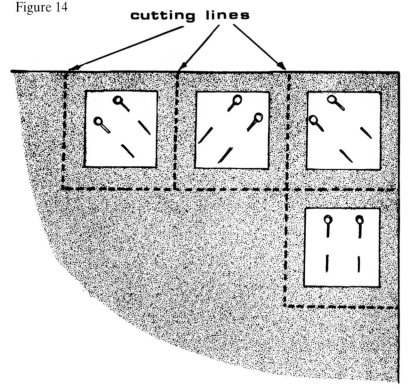

cutting lines

Figure 15

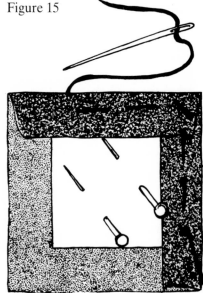

you are working makes it easier to prevent or spot mistakes, and you are less likely to lose pieces.

When all the pieces are covered, you are ready to join them together. Thread a fine needle with strong thread. This thread may be cotton or synthetic and should be of a colour which will blend with your fabrics, though little of it will show. Synthetic threads are strong and come in a wide range of colours, but if you use them remember to take great care when pressing as an iron hot enough to press cotton may melt synthetic threads.

Take one dark square and lay it face down on to the right side of a hexagon, with one side of the square matching up to a long side of the hexagon (figure 16).

Secure your thread with a few running stitches along the fold of the fabric and then start to join the two shapes together with tiny oversewing stitches (figure 17). These stitches should be about 1 mm (1/25 in.) apart, and should pick up a few threads of the material on each patch but should not go through the papers.

When the end of the first side is reached you can finish off your thread with a firm backstitch, or, opening your shapes out flat, you can lay the square on to the next hexagon (figure 18) and stitch them together with fine oversewing stitches. Be sure that you join the hexagons in the correct order.

Once all four hexagons are stitched to the square, the paper in the square patch is removed. This will make it easier to join the short sides of the hexagons together (figure 19).

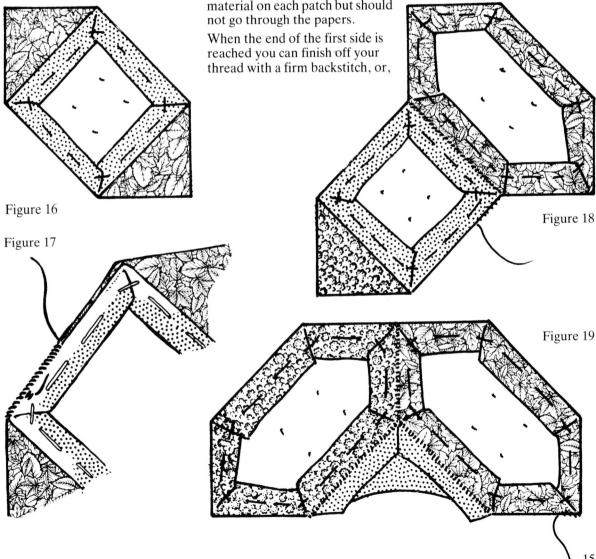

Figure 16

Figure 17

Figure 18

Figure 19

Take particular care when joining the patches to make sure that no holes are left at corners.

Continue to add pieces until your sampler is complete, making sure that your brown and grey hexagons are in their proper positions. As each patch is completely surrounded by other patches the paper template may be removed. If the papers are left in the work will be stiff and difficult to handle as the cushion top grows.

Leave the outside hexagons and triangles with their papers in place until you are ready to make up the sampler into a cushion cover.

CUSHION IN AMERICAN PATCHWORK

The technique referred to as American patchwork does not use paper shapes. Instead, materials are seamed together with running stitches or by machine to form blocks, which are then sewn together to form the pattern. By dividing the central squares into four, and the edging triangles into two, as shown in figure 20, this design can be made up by the American method, using two templates (figure 21).

In order to illustrate more clearly the joins in the central blocks, the arrangement of colours has been changed round in this cushion. (It would be quite possible to make several toning cushions if the colours were switched round, leaving only one as a direct copy of this Venetian floor, the others inspired by it.)

Whilst it would be possible to make the American cushion the same size as the English sample,

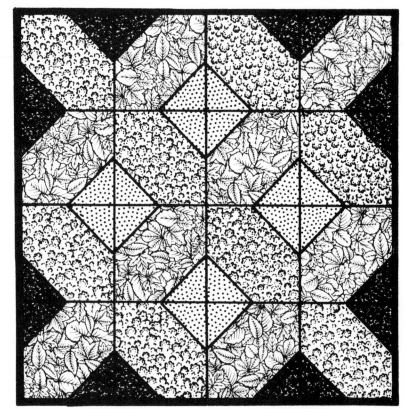

Figure 20

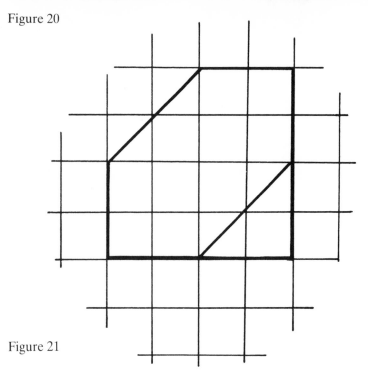

Figure 21

16

small shapes are difficult for a beginner to handle in this technique. This time, let the sides of the squares on the graph paper equal 25 mm (1 in.), resulting in a useful-sized cushion.

When the templates have been drawn out carefully on graph paper (figure 22), glue them on to the back of a piece of sandpaper. When fully dry, cut out carefully using a craft knife and a metal-edged ruler.

Figure 23

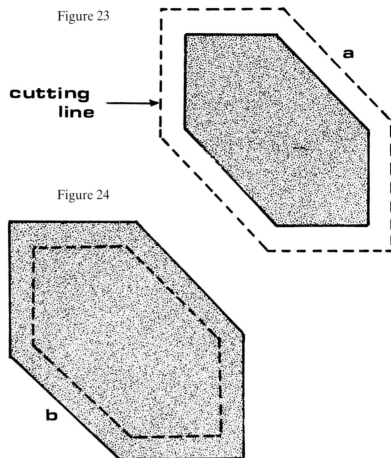

cutting line →

a

Figure 24

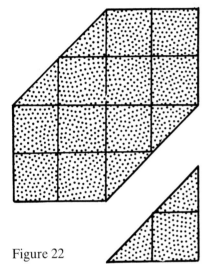

Figure 22

b

There are three methods of making the pattern shapes for American patchwork. Some patchworkers like a template which is the exact size of the finished patch (figure 23). Some like a template the size of the finished patch plus carefully measured turnings (figure 24). Others like to make doubly sure of their measurements by using a window template which gives both the patch size and the seam allowance (figure 25).

Experiment until you find the method you prefer. The window templates are probably best for a beginner, but so much weaker than the other kinds that they

Figure 25

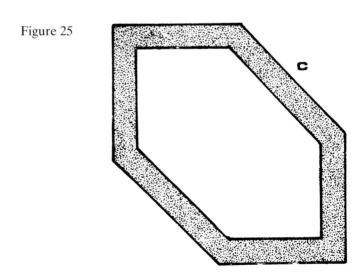

c

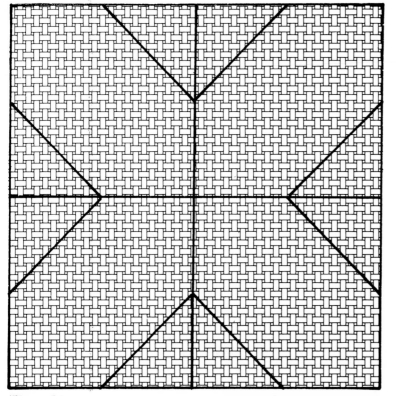

Figure 26

Figure 27

If you have used the template the exact size of the finished patch, cut out leaving adequate seam allowances all around.

If you have used the template which allowed for the seam allowance, cut exactly on the pencilled line.

The third template will have given two lines, one the exact size of the patch, the outer one the cutting line.

It is as important in American patchwork as in English that the grain lines of the fabric should run the same way on all the patches. If you are not careful to ensure this, puckering will result in the finished article.

You want the result shown in figure 26, not that in figure 27.

As for English patchwork, draw out your pattern full size on graph paper and pin it to your pinboarding.

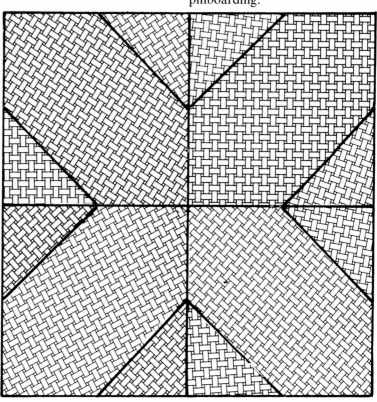

need to be reinforced with stiff card if they are to be used often.

Whichever method you decide to use, take your template and lay it on the wrong side of the appropriate fabric. The fabric should have been well ironed and laid on a smooth table top. The abrasive surface of the sandpaper will hold the template securely in place as you draw around it with a quilter's pencil.

Should the material be too dark for the blue line of the quilter's pencil to show, use a white dressmaker's marking pencil. As this tends to drag the fabric when the point becomes polished with use, be very careful and resharpen the pencil as soon as it starts to catch. Accuracy is absolutely essential so this is not a process to be hurried.

In order to explain clearly the method of making up by the American technique, we will take a hexagon and two triangles of the appropriate colours for the first square in the top left corner.

Cut out, using the window hexagon (figure 28) and triangle templates. You will find that you can mark out very economically if you do not rush.

Place one triangle face down on the right side of the hexagon and, using pins, match up the pencilled lines (figure 29). Pin securely at right angles to the line and then sew along the line by machine, removing the pins as you go. Press the seam open flat (figure 30).

If your measurements and your pencilled lines have been accurate, this should mean that the cut edges also line up exactly, before pressing, and the edge presents a continuous line.

You will now understand why some experienced machinists prefer to dispense with the inner line and rely on accurate marking and cutting of the block using the 'shape plus allowances' template, and their own skilful use of the machine, whilst others prefer not to worry too much about accurate cutting, but pin the block lines carefully and sew accurately along them.

Of course, it is not necessary to use a sewing machine in this technique. In the past all sewing was done by hand using a combination of running and back stitches, but the virtue of the American technique is its speed, and if you are proficient with a sewing machine even a quilt can be made up very quickly.

Complete the first block by placing the other triangle on the opposite side of the hexagon. Pin and stitch into place. Remove all pins and press the seams open flat.

Continue joining sets of three pieces, one hexagon and two triangles, until you have 16 blocks of appropriate pattern, checking each block as you make it against the master design. Pin each completed block into position on your pinboarding (figure 31). Taking the outside block of the top line, and the one next to it, lay them face to face. Pin the

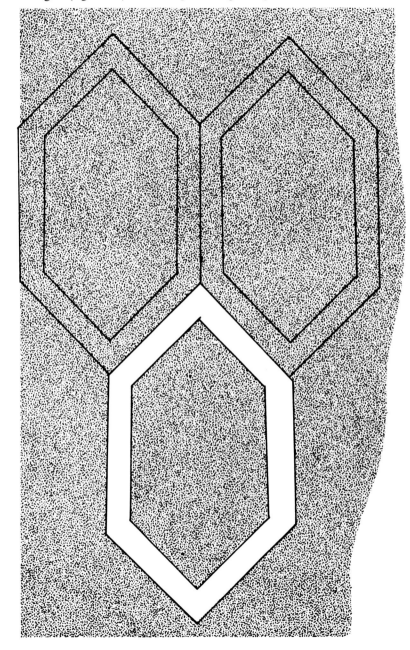

Figure 28

19

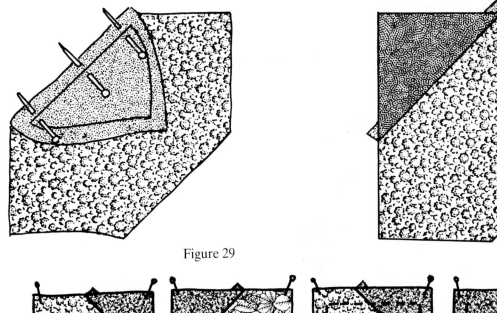

Figure 29

Figure 30

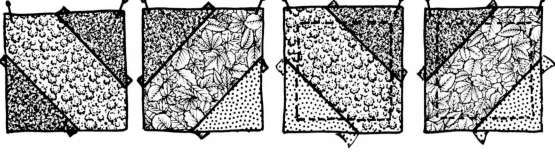

Figure 31

joining line. It is very easy to go wrong here, as when the two blocks are face to face it is only too easy to sew up the wrong side. Pin, then open out to check the correct edges are being fastened together, before sewing (figure 32).

Continue joining the blocks until you have four strips of four.

Join the top strip to the one below it by pinning along the pencilled lines (taking special care to match up the corners). Stitch along this line and press.

Join the third strip and then the fourth strip in the same way.

If the marking out has been accurate, the sewing done as carefully as possible, and each seam pressed with a damp cloth

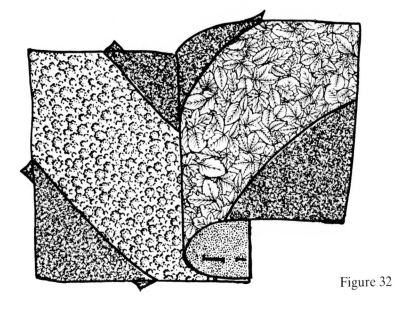

Figure 32

as you worked it, all the joins should match exactly to give as pleasing a result as you have achieved with English patchwork.

MAKING UP THE HERB PILLOW

With the side papers still in place in the English patchwork to hold the shape of the patches, and using a damp cloth, press the cushion top carefully. When it is quite dry, remove the papers along the edges and open out the folds. The pressed line gives you the stitching line when joining the front to the back.

Cut a piece of cotton material the same size as the cushion top, allowing for turnings. This fabric may tone in colour with the materials used in the patchwork, or even be one of the fabrics used. Lay the cushion top face down on the right side of the backing material and pin in place. Machine from about 75 mm (3 in.) from one corner to that corner, turning carefully. Machine along the next three sides, and to about 75 mm (3 in.) from the last corner, leaving an opening of about 50 mm (2 in.) as shown in figure 33.

Turn the cushion cover right side out and check that all the edges look right. If all is correct, turn back and clip the corners so that they will turn out well (figure 34).

The chosen herbs can be put into the resulting sack loose, or in a muslin bag, but in any case the pillow should not be stuffed too full as the herbs are more fragrant when they can be moved about easily. Slipstitch the opening together.

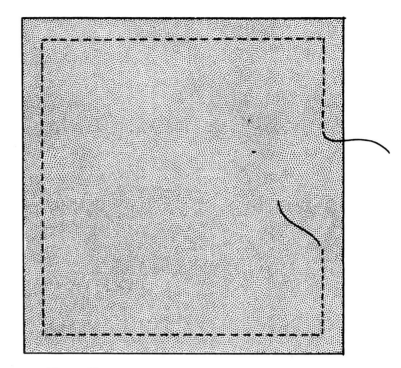

Figure 33

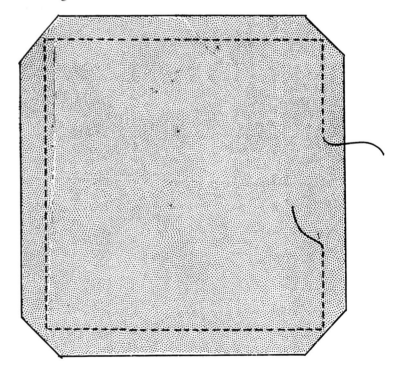

Figure 34

The larger cushion may be
finished in the same way,
although if a cushion pad is to be
put into it, it will be necessary to
leave a much larger opening than
for the herb pillow.

A method of finishing the
opening with a zip fastener will
be shown in Chapter 3.

FURTHER DESIGNS

Figure 35 shows another pattern
from St Mark's where the paviors
quartered the central squares and
halved the outside triangle to
achieve a variation on our first
pattern.

While these designs are very
simple, others which developed
from them make much more
complicated patterns. Figure 36a
shows a corner of another 'quilt'
from St Mark's which has a
second square set diagonally in
the first one. The charts in figure
36b show how to arrive at both
English (a) and American (b)
patchwork templates, with
diagram c being the block for
American patchwork.

Still further variations are found
where the Saltire Cross is twisted
upright, as in the example in
figure 37 from the church of
Madonna del Orto, and the
variation from San Giorgio
Maggiore shown in figure 38.

These patterns can, of course, be
worked perfectly easily by
English patchwork, but, as the
block arrangements for
American patchwork are totally
different, they will be dealt with
in Chapter 7.

Figure 35

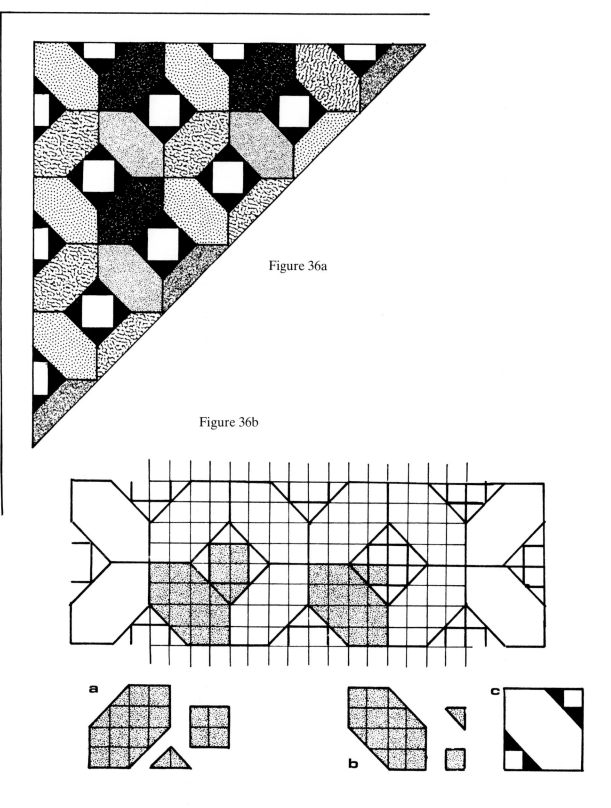

Figure 36a

Figure 36b

Figure 37

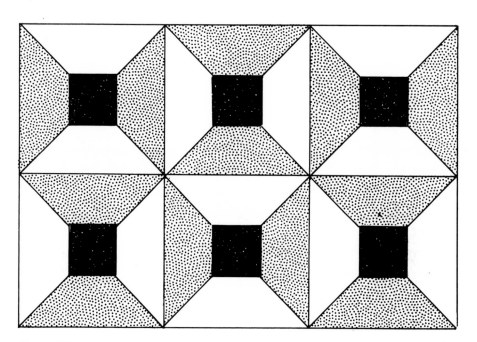

Figure 38

24

2
Materials & Equipment

Having read through Chapter 1, you will have begun to appreciate the range of fabrics and equipment needed to start work as a patchworker. This chapter will act as a summary and a reference.

SEWING EQUIPMENT

FABRICS

Any light- to medium-weight material used for clothing can be used for patchwork. The golden

Figure 39

rule is not to mix fabrics or weights. Keep silks with silks, cotton with cotton, wool with wool. Remember that at some time the article will have to be cleaned and different fibres react in different ways to different methods of cleaning – do not mix them.

The traditional fabric for patchwork is dressweight pure cotton. While polyester/cotton mixes wear as well and wash as well, they are sometimes more difficult to work with and are often not opaque, allowing turnings to show as shadows.

Silk and wool are very pleasant to work with but tend to be expensive. Synthetic fibres are quite acceptable, so long as they are woven, not knitted. Knitted fabrics are very difficult to use for patchwork and should be avoided by the beginner.

It is essential, when making an article which is going to be washed, to ensure that all the fabrics to be used are washed before starting work. This will ensure against possible shrinkage or the running of colour, either of which could be disastrous.

THREADS

Sewing threads should be strong and suit the fibre being used. Ideally, when using cotton fabrics, use cotton thread. Use silk thread with silk or woollen materials.

In practice, synthetic fibre threads work very well, but care must be taken with them when pressing the finished article, as they will melt and ball at a temperature used to press cotton.

Tacking thread should be a soft cotton, easily pulled out. For very fine silks which might mark, use a synthetic or fine silk thread.

SCISSORS

You will need at least two pairs. One will be a pair of dressmaking shears for cutting fabric. The other will be a pair of paper-cutting scissors for cutting paper pattern pieces. Do not use your good shears for paper cutting as they will quickly become blunt. It is also useful to have a small pair of embroidery scissors for snipping the ends of cotton while working.

PINS

Pins should be fine enough not to mark the fabric but yet be easily visible. I use glass-headed pins for patchwork. Their larger cousins, the glass-headed quilting pins obtainable from specialist shops, are invaluable when making up and quilting

NEEDLES

Needles should be as fine as you can use. Sharps or Betweens Nos. 8 or 9 are ideal. If you have difficulty threading these, you may find that Crewel needles, used for embroidery, are easier as they have a longer eye. It is a good idea to thread a number of needles before you start work and put them in a pincushion.

THIMBLES

Few people are taught to use thimbles these days, but when working at English patchwork you will find that your fingertips will suffer unless you use a thimble. When quilting I find that

two thimbles, one on each hand, are essential. Be sure to buy thimbles which fit you comfortably.

MAGNET

You will be working with needles and pins: if you do not need a magnet at some time it will be very surprising!

IRON AND IRONING BOARD

Fabric should have no creases when you start work. In American patchwork it is essential to press each seam as it is completed.

WORK SPACE

The ideal situation is to have a door which can be closed firmly upon work in progress, excluding children and animals! Apart from initial preparation, English patchwork can be done anywhere. American patchwork done by machine requires room to set up sewing machine and ironing board side by side, so one can swivel from one to the other.

MARKING OUT AND DESIGNING EQUIPMENT

A QUILTER'S PENCIL

This is a felt-tipped pen with an ink which vanishes when touched with water, making an ideal medium for marking patterns on light-coloured materials.

DRESSMAKER'S MARKING PENCIL

This chalky pencil is available in white or pale blue. The point tends to polish to a hard surface so it needs to be resharpened frequently.

A CRAFT KNIFE

This should have a thick stock which can be gripped comfortably, and easily changeable blades. If it has a retractable blade, so much the better, especially if there are children about.

A METAL OR METAL-EDGED RULE

It is all too easy to pare slices off a wooden rule with a craft knife.

CUTTING BOARD

Very effective but extremely expensive cutting boards may be purchased. Unless you expect to cut a great many sandpaper templates for patchwork, these are not necessary. An old drawing board or even a kitchen chopping block will do, so long as the surface is reasonably flat and unscored.

SQUARED GRAPH PAPER (figure 40)

This is essential for planning articles made from designs based on a square grid. The article should be drawn to scale, and then the grid used to position the pattern to the best advantage.

It would be possible to use this graph paper for papers for English patchwork, or for drawing the pattern out full size to make templates for American patchwork, but it is much easier to scale the pattern up on to dressmaker's pattern paper (figure 41) and then use that for English papers or American templates.

ISOMETRIC GRAPH PAPER (figure 42)

This is used for planning many of the patterns found in Venice and

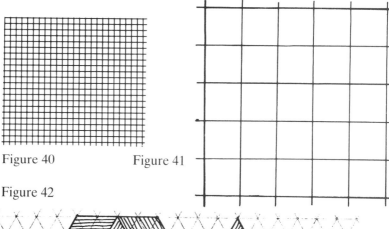

Figure 40   Figure 41

Figure 42

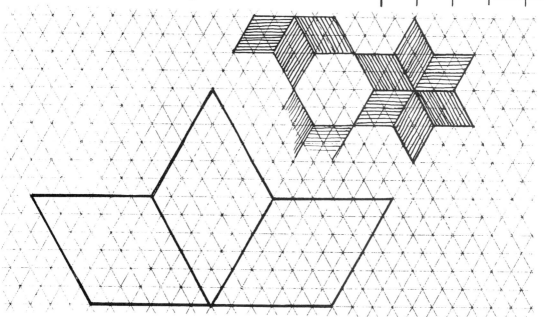

Florence, particularly those based on the hexagon.

Once the design is established, use the same paper for making the papers or templates by scaling up the design as shown.

A particular virtue of using graph paper in this way is that it eliminates the necessity for using templates for most designs in English patchwork. The design is drawn out roughly on to the dressmaker's paper or the isometric paper, and then cut, very accurately, along the printed lines, thus removing one stage where error may creep in.

While most isometric paper on sale is firm enough to make adequate papers for English patchwork, some dressmaker's paper is so flimsy it will need to be glued to something more substantial.

HEAVY CARD OR LIGHT SHEET PLASTIC

Use these for templates for English patchwork as described in Chapter 2.

CARTRIDGE-WEIGHT PAPER

This is for the papers where the English method is being used. American readers: cartridge – weight is roughly construction – paper weight. Stiff four – squares to-the-inch graph paper is also available: see Suppliers.

SANDPAPER GRADE 100

To be used for templates for American patchwork.

COLOURED PENS OR PENCILS

These are helpful when planning designs.

PINBOARDING (BULLETIN = BOARD CORK)

3
Trefoil Design

In our wanderings around Venice, looking for patchwork patterns, one design turned up much more frequently than any other (figure 43). We found it in St Mark's, and also in almost all the later churches, especially those built in the sixteenth and seventeenth centuries, if only as a minor motif on altar steps.

The colours varied from rich reds, golds, and creams to shades of grey, but in any combination of colours it is an attractive and eye-boggling three-dimensional design. Not surprisingly, it is also a well-known pattern in patchwork, though one very seldom sees examples made up.

Figure 43

CUSHION IN TREFOIL DESIGN (see figure 44)

To make a cushion in this design, first decide the size of your basic template, the half-hexagon (figure 45). You need a patch big enough not to be too tiny to work with, and not so big it swamps the design and loses the three-dimensional effect.

Draw out your cushion shape full size on isometric graph paper. This paper is obtainable from stationers who cater for draughtsmen and engineers and it can sometimes be obtained in quite large sheets. If these are not available, join several small ones, making sure that the lines of the design match up perfectly.

Draw three hexagons of the size you have decided upon, with the joining point at the centre of your cushion shape. Bisect each hexagon as shown and colour two half-hexagons a dark colour, two more a medium colour, and leave the third pair white or colour them a very pale tint.

Continue drawing hexagons until you have filled the cushion shape. If the top and bottom edges are not pleasing, make any changes now (Figure 46).

Figure 44

another sheet of isometric paper. You do not need to use a template, as the lines are already there. Proceed to cover the fronts of these papers with your chosen three materials, using the English patchwork method shown in Chapter 1.

Ideally, the grain of the fabric should run the same direction in all the pieces, but this is difficult to accomplish and wasteful of material. Unless the pattern of the fabric dictates that you follow the grain slavishly (a striped material, for instance), it is sufficient to match the grains of the two halves of the hexagon, and this can be achieved by ensuring that the long sides of the half-hexagon lie along the grain of the fabric.

Unless you use the pinboard pattern guide it is all too easy to join the hexagons in the wrong order (figure 48).

Make up a third of the half-hexagons in each of your chosen colours. This done, make hexagons by joining half the darkest pieces to the lightest pieces, and the other half to those in the medium tone. Join the remaining medium-coloured shapes to the remaining light shapes. Pin these hexagons in place on your master design.

You can now start to join the hexagons up into groups of three to make the trefoils, re-placing them on the board when each is completed. Now join the trefoil shapes together, ensuring that they do not become twisted. This may sound very fussy, but it is easy to make a mistake in this pattern. While it is quite possible to unpick patchwork, it is very irritating to have to do so.

Colour in the rest of the trefoils roughly, and pin the sheet to your pinboarding.

It looks as though you should be able to use the two adjoining half-hexagons as one template and save a lot of time and trouble (figure 47). Unfortunately, it is impossible to cover a paper in English patchwork where you have an 'inside' angle, as you would have to snip the fabric in order to catch it over on to the back of the paper. It is, therefore, necessary to make the shape by using two half-hexagon papers.

Cut out a number of half-hexagons the correct size from

Figure 45

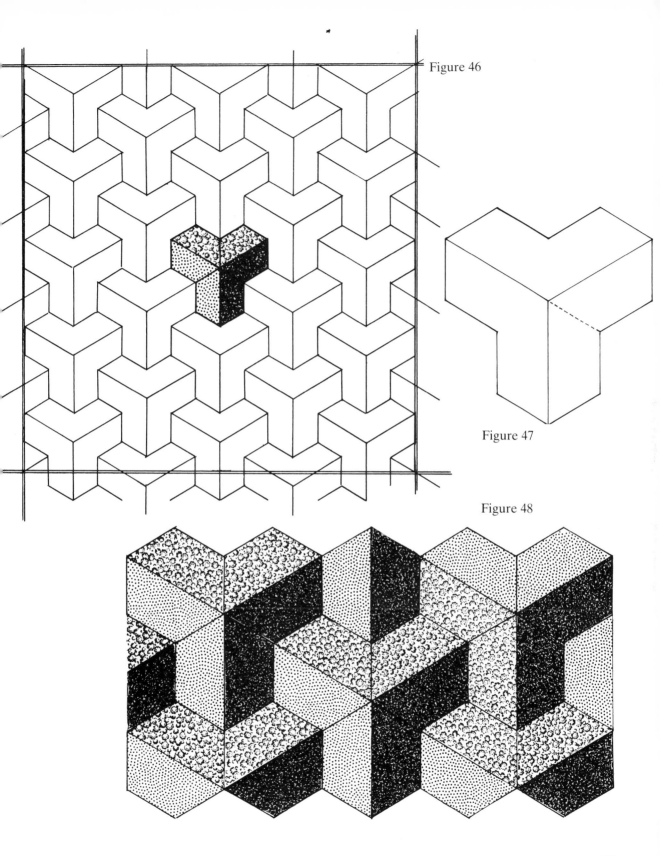

Figure 46

Figure 47

Figure 48

31

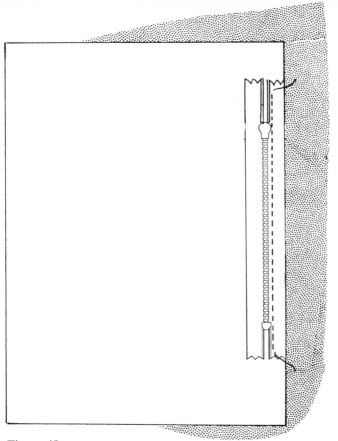

Figure 49

of the zip lying along the edge of the backing. Tack and machine in place (figure 49), and then fold back so the teeth of the zip are just showing.

Press a 40 mm (1½ in.) hem in the second piece of backing, and lay it over the first so that the zip is completely concealed. Tack securely in place.

Machine, from the back, along the fold line until the head of the zip is reached. Make a right-angled turn and sew until the head of the zip is passed. Make another right-angled turn and sew along the teeth of the zip till you

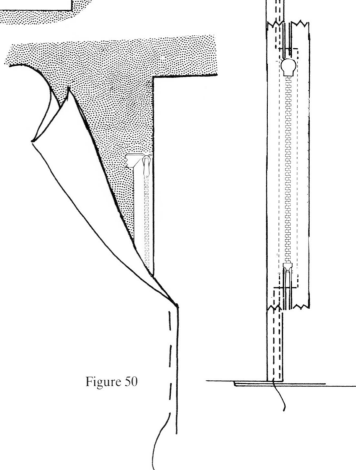

At the edges you will find that you have some shapes which are only parts of the half-hexagon. If these pieces are very small it is usually easier to make up the whole shape and cut it later, rather than fiddle with an awkward pattern piece.

TO MAKE UP THE CUSHION

Take a piece of backing material the width of the cushion top, but 100 mm (4 in.) longer. Cut this in two. Where you cut it will depend on where you wish to position the zip fastener.

Choose a zip fastener 25-50 mm (1-2 in.) shorter than the width of your cushion. Centre it, face down, on the cut edge of one piece of backing, with the fabric

Figure 50

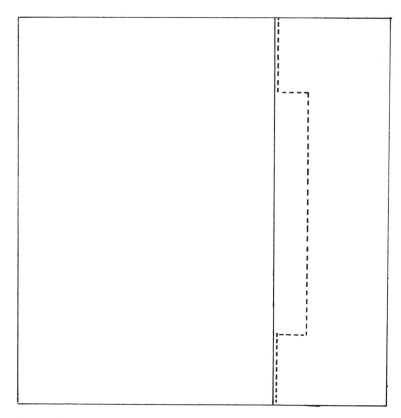

Figure 51

Figure 52

come to the end, when you turn again to go back to the fold line. Turn again and sew along the fold line to the edge (figure 50). Remove the tacking, and you now have a piece of backing with a completely concealed zip fastener (figure 51).

Lay the backing face down on to the right side of the cushion top. Make sure you have the zip undone a little way before you continue, as it is very difficult to undo a zip which is sewn inside a bag!

Tack the two pieces of material together and machine the seams when you have checked that all is well with the design. Remove tacking, clip the corners, and turn the cushion cover right side out (figure 52).

ADAPTING THE PATTERN FOR AMERICAN PATCHWORK (see figure 53)

At first glance it did not seem possible to make this pattern up easily by machine. However, as I like the design very much and wanted to make a single bed quilt using it, I managed eventually to

work out a way in which it could be done. While it would be very much more trouble than English patchwork to do on a small scale, the effort was well worthwhile with the size of patch I used.

To design the quilt, I had first to decide on the final size and then adapt the size of the half-hexagon so that I could get a pleasing repeat. I decided to use a half-hexagon with a long side (a-b) of 230 mm (9 in.) and a short side (b-c) of 115 mm (4½ in.). The quilt was then planned on graph paper with this scale in mind (figure 54).

It would be quite out of the question to pin up a full-size chart of the quilt as was done for the cushion cover, but it is very useful to have the small-scale plan pinned up, and, as each row is finished and connected to the one before, to cross it off on the plan.

I had next to make my templates. To make a quilt by the American technique, it is necessary to join pieces together with straight lines to form blocks which can be assembled with parallel seams. Obviously, the half-hexagons we have used are now useless, and the block I worked out for a repeat is shown in figure 55.

I needed four templates: (a) the half-hexagon, (b) an equilateral triangle whose side is the same as the hexagon, and (c) two rhomboids which are the combined shapes of (a) and (b). These templates were glued to sandpaper and cut out carefully with a craft knife (figure 56).

The fabric was marked, cut out, and assembled as shown in figure 57. To make the diagrams clearer the sewing lines have been shown as though they were marked on the front of the material.

Figure 53

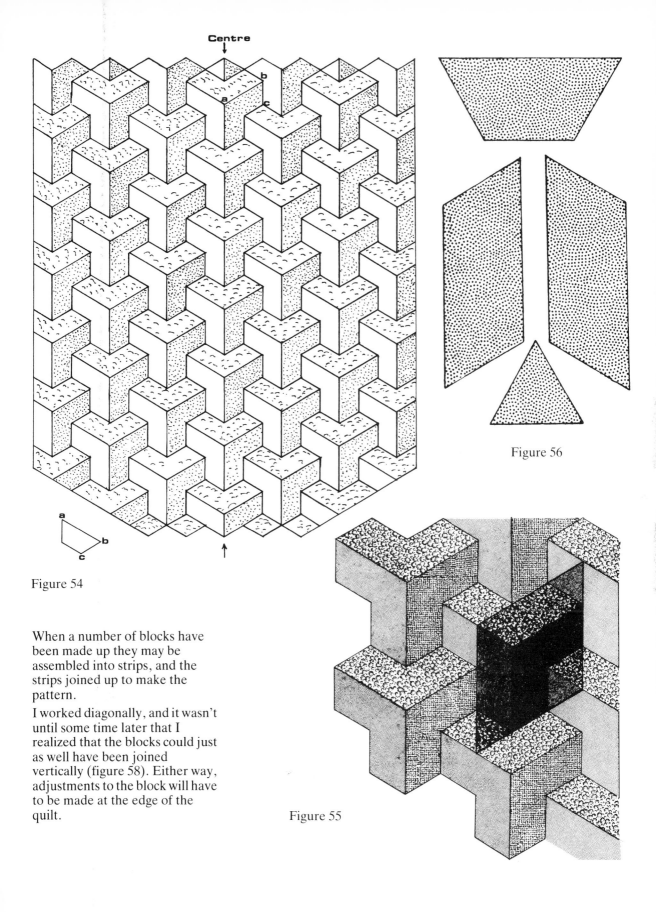

Centre

b

a

c

a

b

c

Figure 54

Figure 56

Figure 55

When a number of blocks have been made up they may be assembled into strips, and the strips joined up to make the pattern.

I worked diagonally, and it wasn't until some time later that I realized that the blocks could just as well have been joined vertically (figure 58). Either way, adjustments to the block will have to be made at the edge of the quilt.

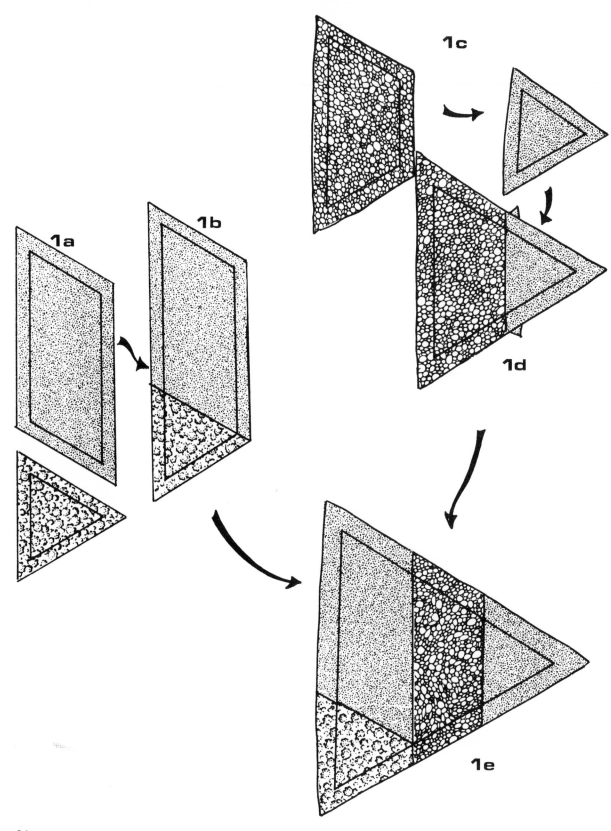

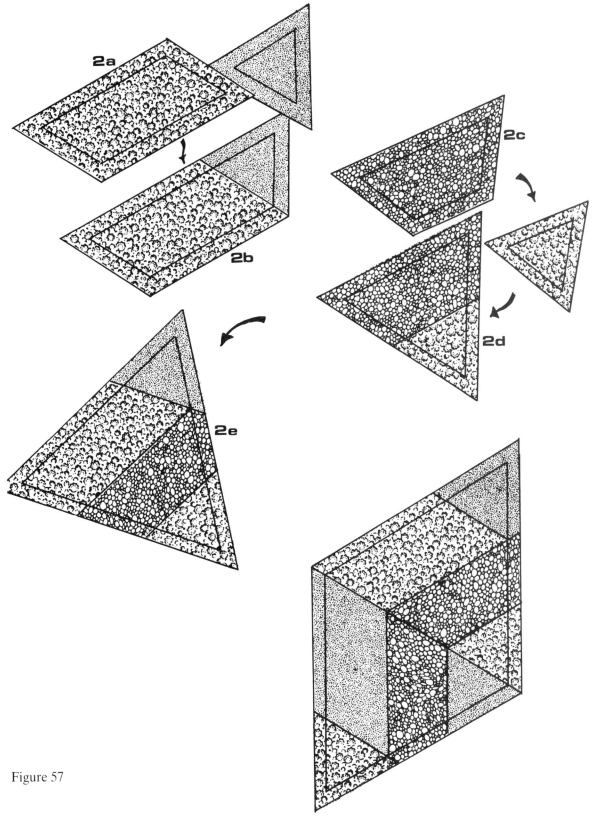

2a

2b

2c

2d

2e

Figure 57

37

Figure 58

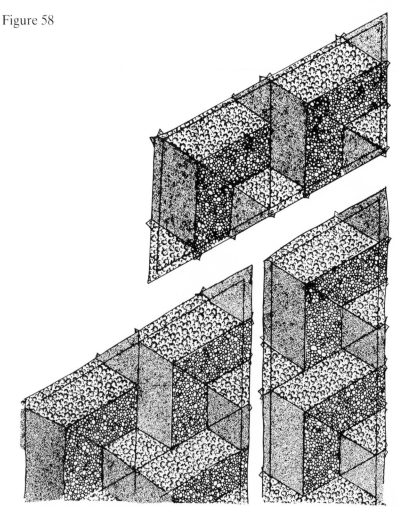

Figure 59 shows the first three rows marked off in the diagonal method I used, but also shows how it could be worked using vertical rows.

In Chapter 5 you will find methods of putting a quilt together dealt with in detail. In this case, I used a backing material which was considerably larger than the patchworked top. I laid wadding[1] of the correct size on the backing and centred it, and then folded the edges of the backing over and tacked them into place, mitring the corners. The patched top was then hemmed down on to the edges thus formed before quilting. The quilt was then quilted by hand, as described in Chapter 5.

[1]American readers: batting

Figure 59

HOLLOW LATTICE DESIGN
(see figure 60)

While we collected a number of isometric patterns, only one other lends itself easily to manufacture by the American method. This is the hollow lattice design, shown in figure 61, which we found on a pavement in St Mark's and also on the Golden Staircase in the Doge's Palace (figure 62). In St Mark's the pattern was tiny, but the much later staircase had blocks with sides of approximately 300 mm (12 in.)

It is worth mentioning that, while I have shown no dimensions on the drawings in the book, we found the same patterns with repeats varying from 50-600 mm (2 in.-2 ft).

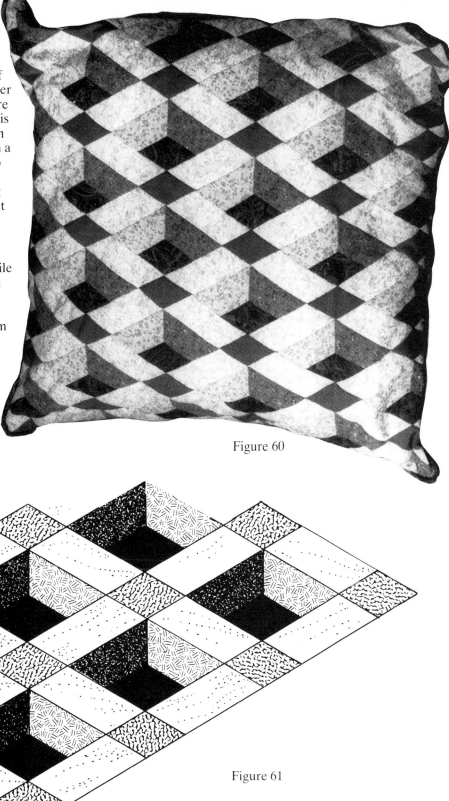

Figure 60

Figure 61

Figure 62

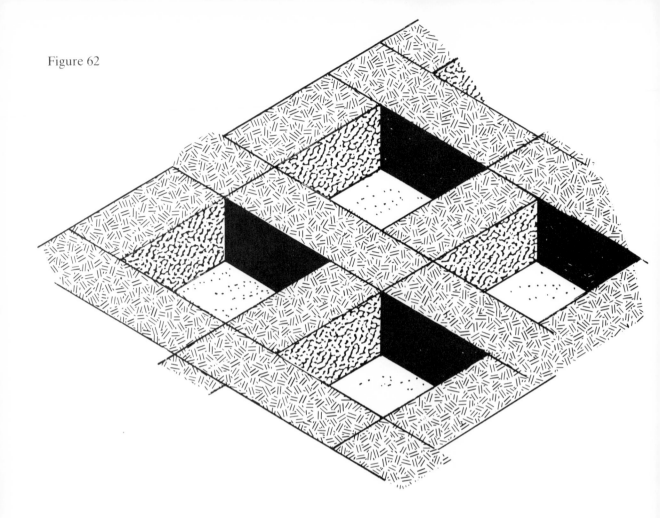

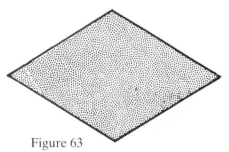

Figure 63

The block and templates for this method are shown in figure 63. In fact, the only additional template to those shown for the trefoil pattern is the rhombus formed by joining two of the triangle templates. The block for

the lattice pattern is shown in figure 64, together with the method of assembly (figure 65).

For the design from the Doge's Palace, the strip C could be one piece, or could continue all across the article being made up.

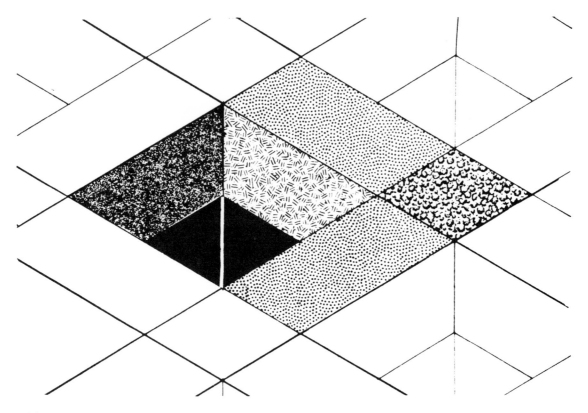

Figure 64

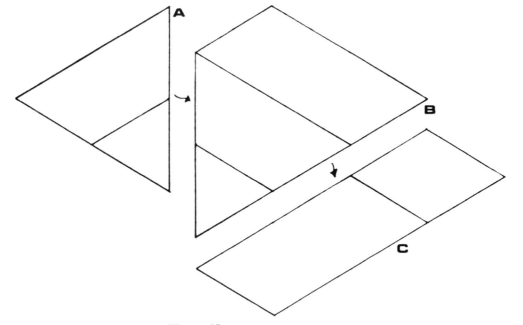

Figure 65

4

More Isometric Designs

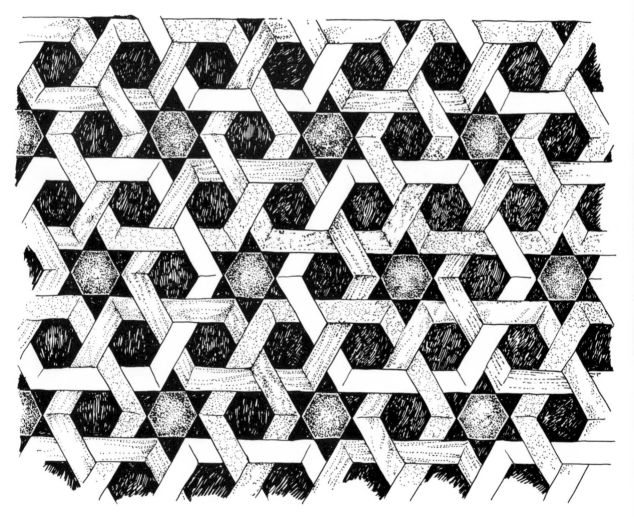

Figure 66

Many of the patterns we found in Venice, and, later, in Tuscany, were based on isometric projection, where the construction lines are at 60° to one another. In the last chapter a few such patterns were described, but we found many, many more.

ISOMETRIC GRID DESIGNS

Most frequently, the designs we saw were those based on a combination of hexagons and triangles. The small floor shown in figure 66 was found in St Mark's Cathedral. It is so complicated that while it could be adapted for machine patchwork (as the designs in Chapter 3 were adapted) it is probably better to reserve it, and others like it, for the English method worked over papers (figure 67), and for small articles which will not take too long to make.

SEWING CASE

A very useful item to make as a gift (or, for that matter, to keep for oneself) is a travelling sewing case in which scissors, thimble, needles and an adequate supply of threads can be carried. A design from the floor of a chapel in the Monastery of Certosa di Val d'Ema (just outside Florence) would lend itself well for this purpose (figure 68).

In the original floor the long hexagons had 350 mm (12 in.) sides and were of red, black and green marble, while the triangle was a warm buff stone.

When designing a pattern for the sewing case, it is best *not* to start

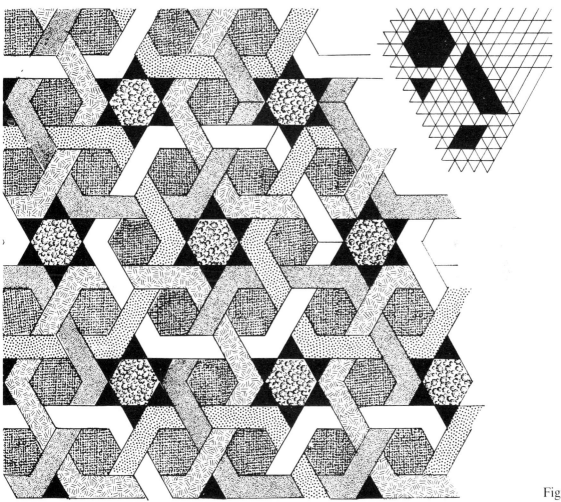

Figure 67

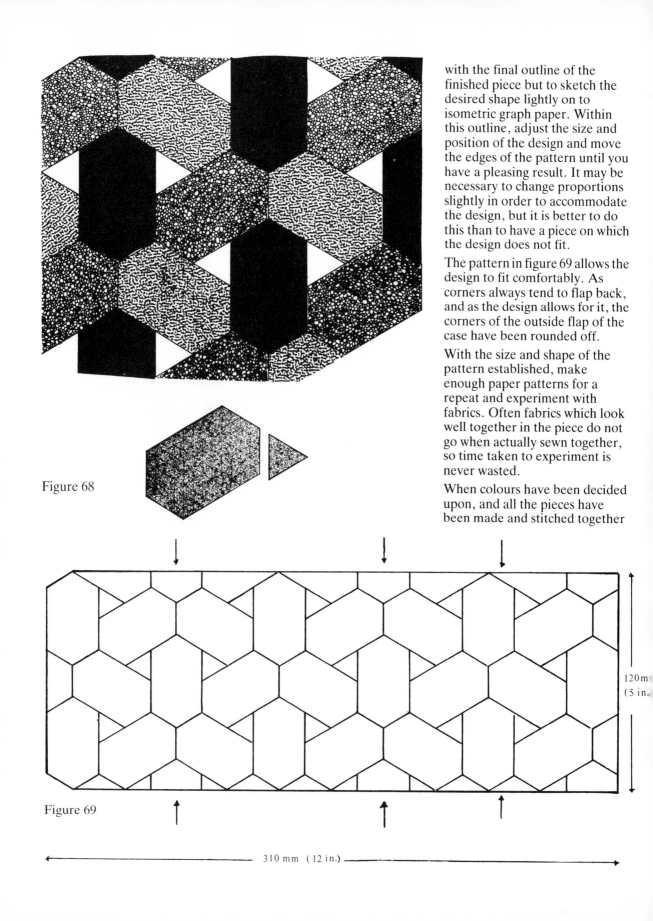

with the final outline of the finished piece but to sketch the desired shape lightly on to isometric graph paper. Within this outline, adjust the size and position of the design and move the edges of the pattern until you have a pleasing result. It may be necessary to change proportions slightly in order to accommodate the design, but it is better to do this than to have a piece on which the design does not fit.

The pattern in figure 69 allows the design to fit comfortably. As corners always tend to flap back, and as the design allows for it, the corners of the outside flap of the case have been rounded off.

With the size and shape of the pattern established, make enough paper patterns for a repeat and experiment with fabrics. Often fabrics which look well together in the piece do not go when actually sewn together, so time taken to experiment is never wasted.

When colours have been decided upon, and all the pieces have been made and stitched together

Figure 68

Figure 69

120 mm
(5 in.)

310 mm (12 in.)

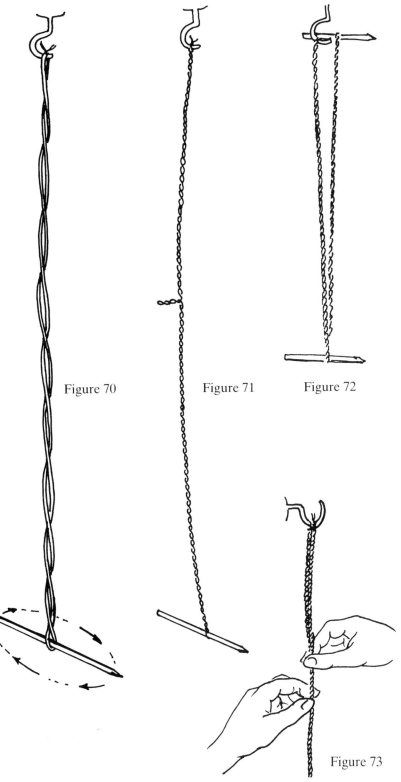

Figure 70

Figure 71

Figure 72

Figure 73

(see Chapter 2 for method), quilt the cover with tiny running stitches on to a backing of heavy-duty Vilene with a layer of 50 g (2 oz) synthetic wadding between the patchwork and the stiff back layer. As the work is very small, and quilting outside the seam line would make for fussiness, quilt 'in the ditch', i.e. along the seamlines of the patchwork. As you quilt, sew the raw edges of the outside patches over on to the back of the Vilene.

When the quilting is complete, take a suitable piece of cotton poplin, 6 mm (¼ in.) larger in all dimensions than the quilted cover, and pin it to the back of the Vilene. Turn in the raw edges and slip stitch the folded edges of the poplin and the patchwork together. This may not provide a perfect edge, and an alternative is to make a cord using stranded cotton matching one of the colours of the fabrics, and apply it around the edges to hide unevenness of join or stitches.

TO MAKE A CORD

Take a length of stranded cotton roughly three times the desired length of the finished cord. Knot the ends together and secure it on a hook, keeping the knot at the hook. Slip a pencil into the loop so formed, pull the loop taut, and commence winding the double thread by rotating the pencil (figure 70).

When you think the cord is twisted enough, slack off slightly. If the cord is wound enough it will begin to double back on itself at the centre (figure 71).

Holding the cord stretched and taut, double it (a friend is helpful here) and slide the loop from the pencil over the hook (figure 72).

Now, starting with the doubled end, slide out the second pencil with which you have been holding it taut, and release the cord, 2 cm (1 in.) or so at a time, until you reach the hook (figure 73). Slide the loops off the hook and knot them together. You should have a neat, tightly twisted, even cord.

Scissors tend to slide out of sewing cases with distressing ease. In this case, one end is turned over and stitched down to form a pocket to hold them, and a thimble, securely, the stitching being extended up the side of the overlap more than halfway (A–B). When sewing the pocket in place, leave gaps at A, D and E to thread the cord in.

Anchor the knotted end of the cord inside the pocket at A, and thread the cord through the hole left for it. Stitch it in place from A to B, and then along the loose edge B-C, anchoring it firmly at the corner C. Take the cord inside the pocket to D, then bring it out through the hole left at the corner and sew it down on the edge of the case from D back to C. Continue all around the edge of the case to E, then thread the cord into the pocket again and secure it (figure 74).

Fold the loose end of the case over to make an envelope until the patterns line up (figure 75). Pin in place. Position snap fasteners, sewing them down with threads which match the fabrics on which they are positioned.

Stitch a folded piece of felt, which has been trimmed to fit with pinking shears, into position on the new fold. This will hold the pins and needles.

In the space between the stitching line for the felt and the pocket for the scissors, stitch two rows of tape, matching, if possible, the poplin you have used for the lining. (If you cannot find matching tape, choose a strongly contrasting colour – better a strong contrast than a missed match.)

Place the tapes so that they will hold a number of small reels of cotton or silk – the spaces will depend on the threads you wish to use. Elastic can be used instead of tape, but it is more difficult to finish the ends neatly with elastic – the best way is to sandwich the ends between the layers of material when the lining is being sewn in place. Figure 76 shows the finished case.

SMALL BAG

Another very useful item to make is a little bag to hold makeup, pencils, or other small things which need to be kept together. This time the design chosen is one found in St Mark's in Venice and in the Baptistry in Florence.

Make up the design exactly as shown in figure 77, letting the side of the hexagon be 20 mm (¾ in.). Fold the resulting shape in half where the arrows indicate, right sides together. Join the ends of the bag by stitching the three diamonds on one side to the hexagons on the other, thus making a small, shallow bag. Remove all papers, turn to the right side and press. You will have a very neat little bag with rounded bottom corners.

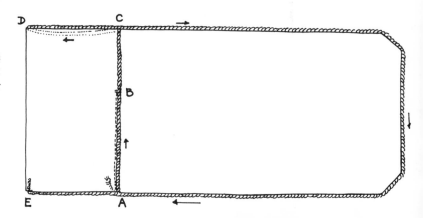

Figure 74   Figure 75

Stitch a 180 mm (7 in.) dress zip fastener into the top of the bag, tucking the fabric ends inside and making sure that the folded-over fabric and the stitches are well away from the teeth of the zip.

Make a lining bag slightly smaller than the patchwork one and slide it into place. Fold over the top edges and stitch them to the fabric of the zip, even further from the teeth than the original row of stitches.

There are several variations on this hexagon and diamond design, the simplest being the one shown in figure 79 which was found in the Baptistry in Florence. An even more effective one from St Mark's is shown in figures 80 and 81. This would also lend itself easily to manufacture by machine.

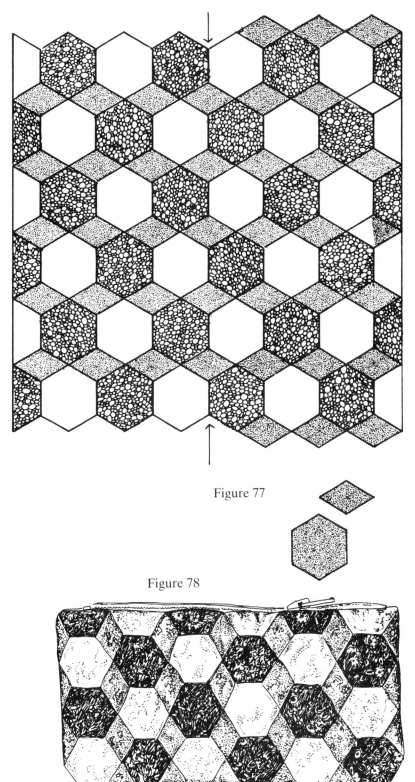

Figure 76

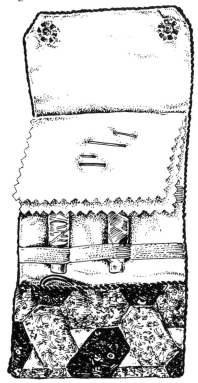

Figure 77

Figure 78

Figure 79

Figure 81

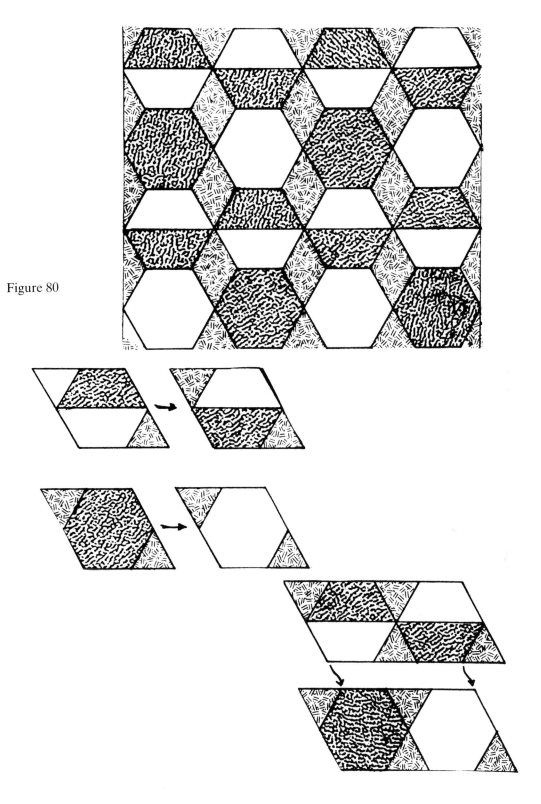

Figure 80

5

Tumbling Blocks

The 'tumbling blocks' or 'baby's blocks' pattern (figure 82), so well known to patchworkers, is found in Venice as whole floors, as altar steps, or as a small pattern infill.

Even more interesting are the variations on the theme. Figure 83 shows one from the church of Santa Spirito in Florence and the further complication (figure 84) is from the floor of Santa Maria della Salute in Venice where, by slightly varying the angles of the blocks, the design is made to spiral into the centre of the floor in ever-diminishing rows of glowing colour.

Both these designs could be worked by machine in vertical stripes, as indicated.

Two more designs based entirely on diamonds are figure 85, making interconnecting hexagons, and figure 86, a variation on tumbling blocks from St Mark's.

Even the very simple angled chequerboard from the Baptistry in Florence (figure 87) is effective, while the border from Orsanmichele in the same city (figure 88), which could be extended as shown, is even more attractive.

Hexagons and triangles were used to make the pattern shown in figures 89 and 90 from the church of San Niccolo da Tolentini in Venice.

St Mark's yielded another eye-dazzling grid (figure 91) and in San Pietro da Castillo, a lovely church hardly known to tourists, though it was till quite recently the Cathedral of Venice, we found this elongated version of the tumbling blocks (figure 92).

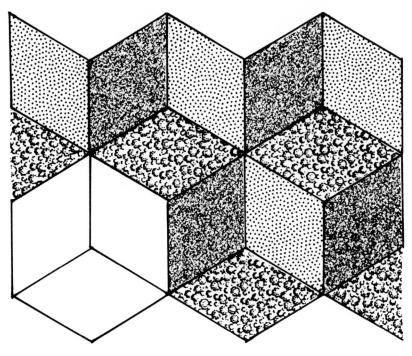

Figure 82

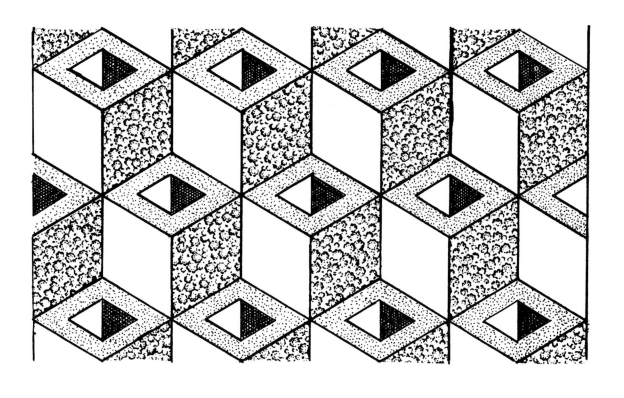

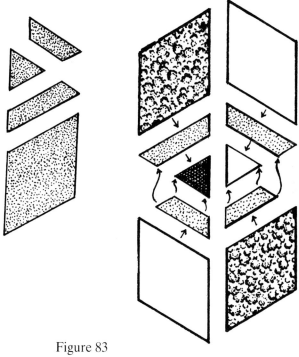

Figure 83

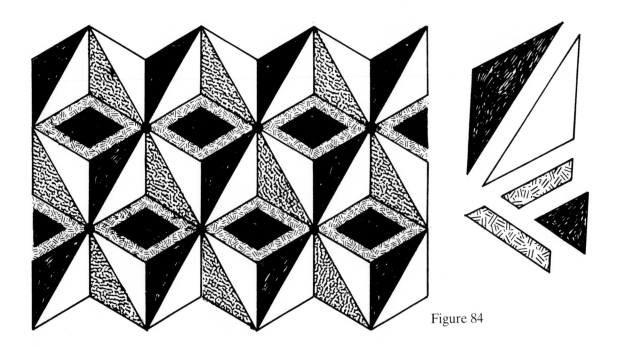

Figure 84

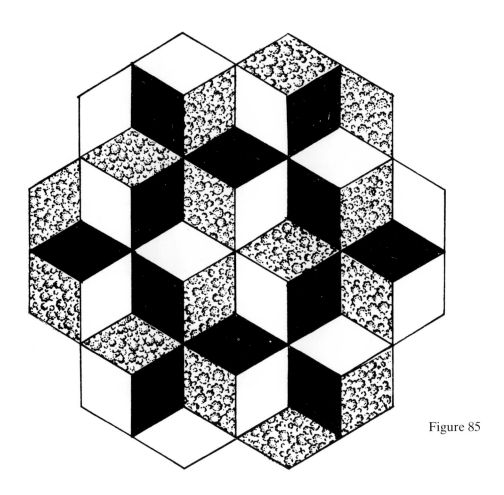

Figure 85

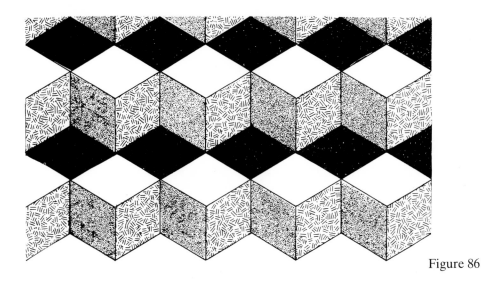

Figure 86

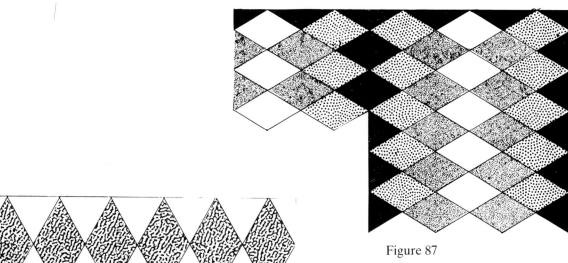

Figure 87

Figure 88

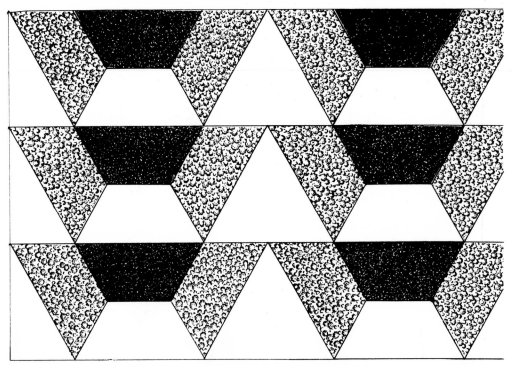

Figure 89

Figure 90

Figure 91

Figure 92

55

Figure 93

CAVALIER TUMBLING BLOCKS

When you draw the tumbling blocks pattern on a square grid instead of using isometric paper, you arrive at a whole new vocabulary of patterns. The lozenge facing you becomes a square in cavalier projection, and the top and side lozenges become rhomboids. This pattern, with the rhomboids of many differing dimensions, is found in many Venetian buildings.

These patterns were frequently further decorated, as in figure 93, which comes from a border at the main entrance to St Mark's Basilica, where it glows with warm honey tones, deepening to umber, and set off with black.

In its simplest form, as in this example from the splendid floor in San Giorgio Maggiore in

Venice (figure 94), the design could easily be worked by machine if the squares were cut into two triangles and the pattern joined diagonally.

Figure 94

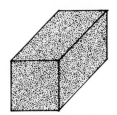

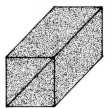

56

The even squarer version in figure 95 comes from the splendidly Baroque church of the Gesuiti, where it adorns some altar steps in black, yellow and white and others in white, red and yellow.

Figure 95

Occasionally the design is found reversed, as in figure 96, while a further row of square blocks (which would also have to be cut in half diagonally for machine patchwork) introduces an additional element into the design (figure 97). Another pattern (figure 98), like the first from St Mark's, introduces yet more complication.

The design on p.59 breaks down simply for English patchwork (figure 99), and dividing the central black square into equal triangles facilitates easy manufacture by machine. It would be very difficult, however, to make it up to the original size of the pavement, where the squares measured just under 8 cm (3 in.) a side.

Figure 96

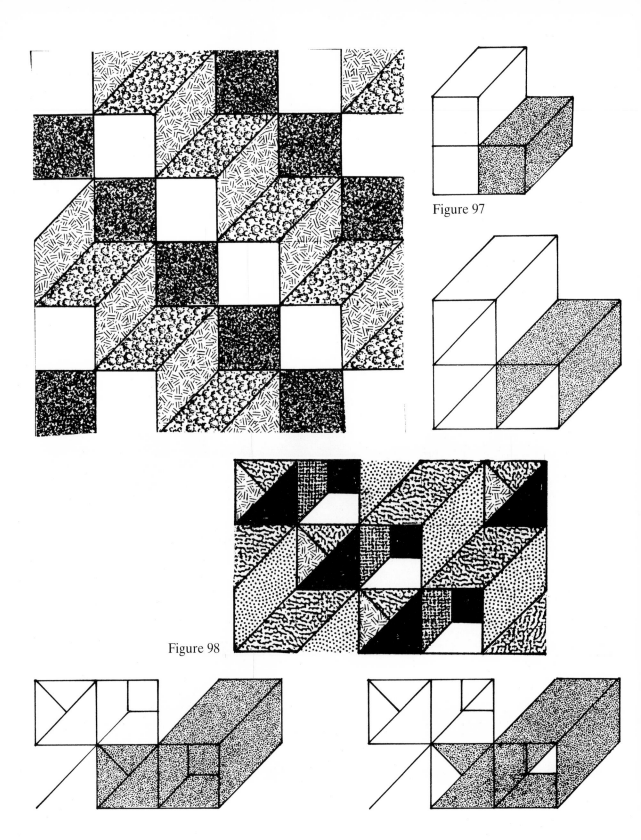

Figure 97

Figure 98

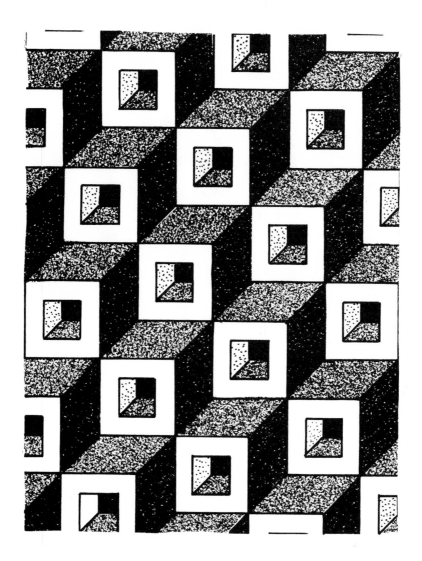

Figure 99

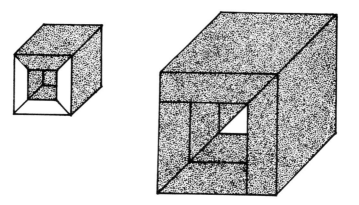

QUILT FROM SANTA MARIA MIRACOLI

While all these patterns are attractive, the one which completely captivated us was that from the upper floor in the exquisite little church of Santa Maria Miracoli, where the cavalier tumbling block theme was carried to extravagant lengths (figure 100) in glowing creams, yellows, blue greys and reds (101 shows the full repeat). This floor, dated 1481, has squares measuring 30 cm (12 in.) a side. It seemed perfect for a quilt.

The quilt was planned, as shown in figure 102, using a 230 mm (9 in.) block, since the size of the block in the original floor seemed too large for a quilt. The quilt was designed for a large single bed (1 x 2 m [40 x 80 in.]) where corners dragging on the floor would be a hazard. Happily, the design made cutting the corners off very easy.

Although a casual glance would indicate that the templates required for the dark rhomboid are the same as for the light one, they are in fact reversed, so two sets of templates are required (figure 103).

Draw the templates out very accurately on dressmaker's graph paper and glue the pieces to the back of fine sandpaper, with the positions labelled. Cut the templates with a craft knife and a steel rule.

When choosing the fabrics for the quilt, it is not necessary to stick to the basic five fabrics. So long as the blues, for example, are of a similar tone value and scattered about the quilt in a random fashion (which means, of course, careful planning), several fabrics can be used. Such a decision

Figure 100

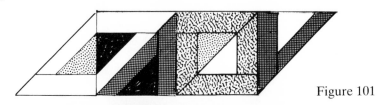

Figure 101

Figure 102

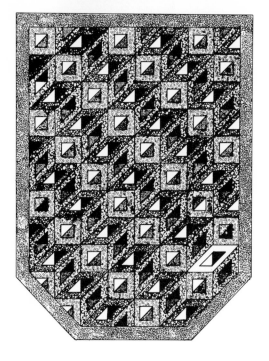

60

1 Wall hanging taken from a small
floor pattern in the atrium of
St Mark's. Chapter 12

2 Blue silk bag in hexagon design with applied pegs. Chapter 10

3 Bag and sewing case using isometric designs. Chapter 4

4 Three cushions based on isometric patterns. Chapters 3 and 4

5 Cushions using curved lines and complicated patterns. Chapter 11

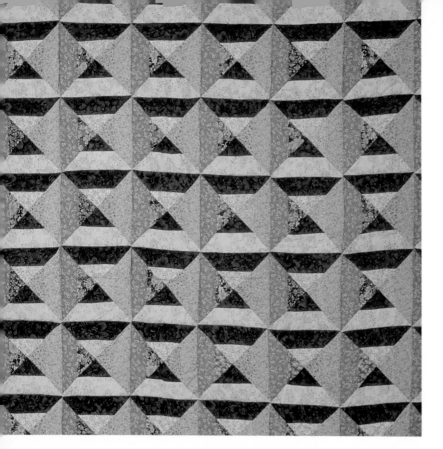

6 Design from the entrance to St Mark's. Chapter 7

7 *(Bottom left)* Design from the church of San Zaccaria. Chapter 8

8 *(Bottom right)* Design from Santa Maria Miracoli. Chapter 5

Figure 103

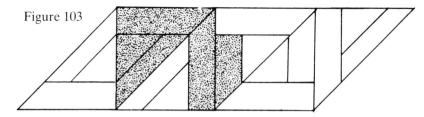

would depend on availability of material as well as aesthetics. The centres would need to be kept standard to hold the design together.

It was at this time that I made a very silly but common mistake. I marked out and cut all the browns which I was using for the dark rhomboid, and then found that I had not thought through the process of marking and cutting. Because the smooth side of the sandpaper is marked, but the rough side pressed to the wrong side of the fabric, it is necessary to reverse the design when drawing it out on the graph paper if it is to be cut correctly. In most designs this does not matter, but in the Santa Maria Miracoli

pattern it is vital. I could not cut all the browns again, so my quilt is a mirror image of the Santa Maria Miracoli floor!

Although the quilt could be assembled diagonally, as were the trefoils in the first quilt, I found it convenient to assemble mine horizontally (figure 104). Because of the size of the repeat it went together very quickly.

The backing of the quilt can be made of cotton fabric of a similar weight to the pieces used for the patchwork, but if cloth is bought by the metre it will have to be joined, leaving seamlines down the length of the quilt. I prefer, where possible, to buy a coloured sheet or wide sheeting material in an appropriate colour and to

avoid the joining seams.

In areas where there are specialist patchworker's and quilter's suppliers (see p.141) it is possible to buy quilt batts made of cotton or synthetic wadding in various sizes and weights. Buy one larger than your quilt and trim it to a few inches larger than your top all around.

If purpose-made quilt batts are not available, make your own by purchasing wadding off the roll and tacking the slightly overlapped edges together. This works quite well but obviously is not quite so satisfactory as the full width piece.

Before starting to make up the quilt, the backing should be washed until all possibility of colour running is eliminated. Press the sheeting and ensure that the grain is true – that warp and weft are at right-angles throughout.

Lay the sheeting out flat on the floor. (If the floor is carpeted, so much the better as there will be

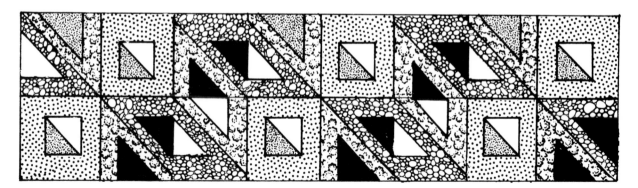

Figure 104

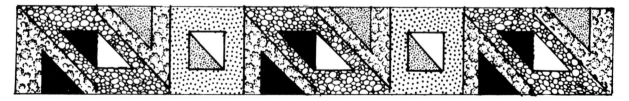

61

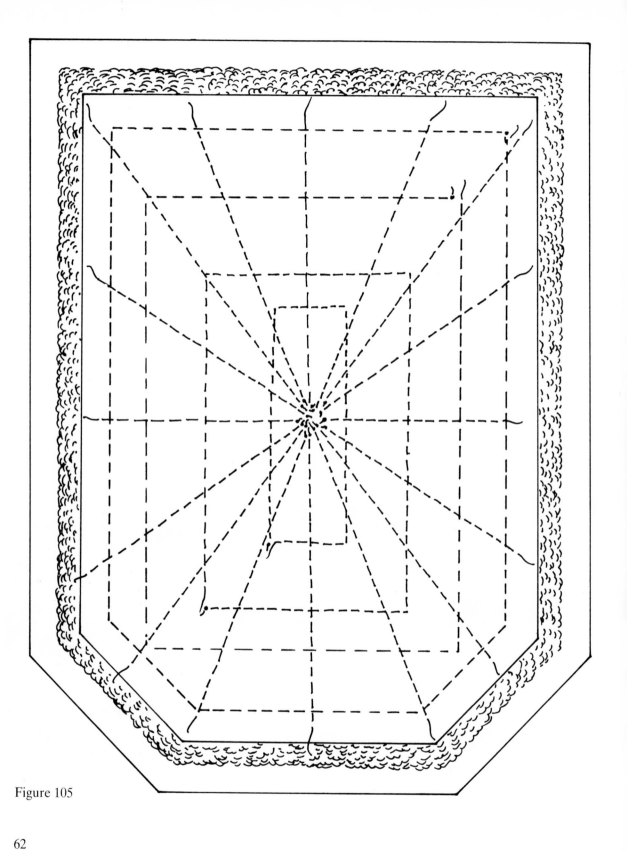

Figure 105

less risk of movement.) The wadding is next laid on the sheeting, and the patchwork spread over, face up, and positioned carefully.

Pin the three thicknesses together with glass-headed quilter's pins (longer than dressmaking pins). I find that glass-headed pins are harder to overlook later than ordinary dressmaker's pins.

The three thicknesses must now be tacked together. There is no doubt that this process is the most tedious part of making the quilt. The temptation to skimp is very strong but must be resisted, as the success of the quilting depends upon meticulous care at this stage.

Start at the centre and work out to the edges, as shown in figure 105.

When the 'spokes' have been tacked, the rectangles are tacked in, working out from the centre.

Length of stitch is not very important, so long as the three thicknesses are caught together each time. Stitches 50 mm (2 in.) are quite adequate, and the row of stitches need not be finished off.

It is at this stage that I trim the batt and the backing, the first to 100 mm (4 in.) from the edge of the patchwork, and the lining a further 150 mm (6 in.) beyond that, but others prefer to cut each to size before putting the three layers together.

The extra material from the backing is now folded to the front, enclosing the exposed edge of the batt, and tucked under the patchwork. Mitres are pinned at the corners, and then the patchwork tacked into position (figure 106).

QUILTING ON A HOOP

Lack of space in the house where I lived when I made this quilt made it impossible to set up a proper quilting frame, so I made do with a large quilting hoop – like an embroiderer's tambour hoop, only deeper (figure 107).

This works well if care is exercised when moving from one section to another to ensure that no puckers or folds appear in the backing. (If the pinning and tacking have been thorough there should be no problem.)

The main difficulty with a hoop is manipulating the rolls of unquilted patchwork and batting while attempting to start quilting at the centre. It is no job for a hot day!

Quilting serves two purposes: it holds the layers of material firmly together and prevents the batt from slipping to one side or one end, and it is decorative. As the synthetic batt traps air in its interstices it is very warm, and to quilt it tightly in patterns would diminish the warmth of the quilt, so I merely quilted the main outlines of the shapes, along the seamlines.

The thread used was a strong quilting cotton. This can be obtained in a full range of colours from specialist shops, or No. 40 Sewing Cotton will do. A light stroke with a beeswax block will make knotting less likely as you work.

Quilting can be stab stitched on a taut ground (figure 108), or the thicknesses of material can be eased slightly in the frame, and running stitches taken, two or three on a needle at a time. While stab stitching is neater, it is very slow and, for a quilt, running stitches are much more practical.

It is useful to have several needles threaded before you start. Knot the thread securely and put your needle into the top fabric a little way from where you intend to start your run of stitches. This knot may either be left on the surface and cut off later, or pulled sharply so that it goes through the patchwork and lodges between the layers of material. The method used depends on the fabric you are using – the knot would be left on the surface on silk, for instance.

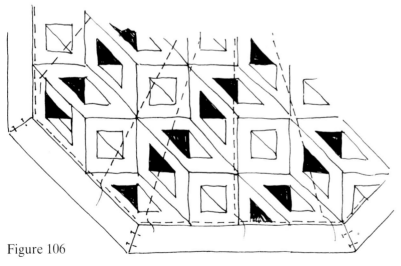

Figure 106

At the start of the run, take a backstitch to anchor the thread, and then start to stitch. The size of stitches should be constant but need not be too small. I have read of a quilting group who will only admit to their membership those who can quilt ten stitches to the inch (2.5 cm), but you will see quilts at exhibitions where the stitches are three to the inch.

If you are right-handed, keep the left hand under the quilt to guide the needle as it comes through. There are various finger guards on the market to prevent this being a bloody procedure, but I find a thimble on each hand sufficient.

When you come to the end of the thread, take a backstitch and lose the end of the thread within the thickness of the quilt. After the centre has been quilted, move the hoop towards the edge, and continue till you have worked all around the area first quilted.

When all the patchwork has been quilted, instead of hemming the quilt top to the backing material which has been folded to the front to form a border, attach the patchwork by quilting, through all thicknesses, sewing just inside the folded edge of the patchwork.

The edge of the wadding may be inclined to roll if left loose, so it is useful to quilt the border in a pattern, even so simple a one as a zigzag.

As a final touch, do embroider your name and the date on the top of the quilt, either on the outside of the border or on the inside. Someone in the future might well be interested.

N.B. It is worthwhile looking at the designs in this chapter from different angles when planning a quilt or cushion, as often they present quite a different effect when viewed from another angle.

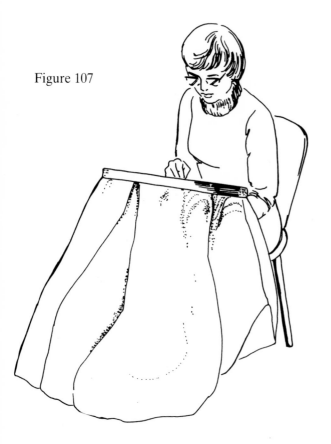

Figure 107

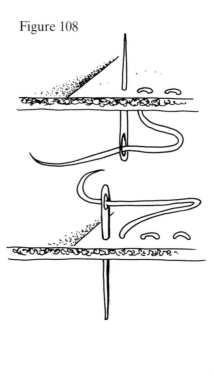

Figure 108

6

Hollow Squares

The three-dimensional effect provided by a hollow square was a favourite design in Venice. Based on isometric projection, we met it on pp.39-41 in Chapter 3, and p.54 in Chapter 5, but it was quite as popular when based on the square grid.

ADAPTING DESIGNS

One of the oldest versions we found was that shown in figure 109 in an 800 year old floor in SS Maria and Donato in Murano. This very attractive pattern can be used in English patchwork with ease but is also easily adapted for American patchwork

by using vertical strips (figure 110).

In its simplest form (from the main floor of Santa Maria Formosa in Venice) the hollow square makes a very satisfactory pattern (figure 111).

The design in figure 112, from St Mark's, shows the same repeat

Figure 109

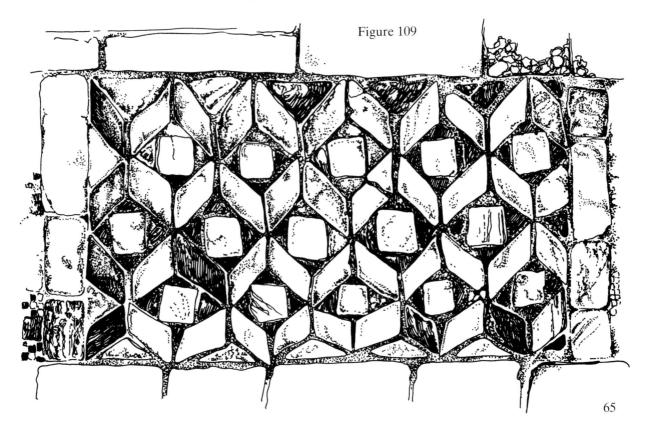

given a quarter turn to the diagonal, with the addition of spacing bars. Both designs could be adapted for machine patchwork by dividing the squares diagonally.

Again from St Mark's, two more rows of pattern are added to achieve a more complicated design (figure 113). By working in vertical strips, and cutting the central square into two triangles, this could, if the pattern were large enough, easily be worked by machine.

By squashing the shape, the paviors in St Mark's achieved a pattern so nearly like the traditional tumbling blocks that it is necessary to check angles carefully to be sure that a square grid and not isometric projection was used to achieve the design (figure 114).

Two further elaborations of the design, both from St Mark's, are shown in figures 115 and 116. While it would be quite possible to work the first example by machine, the second is so complicated that the effort would barely be worthwhile.

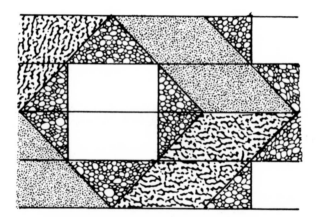

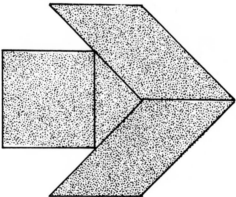

Figure 110

Figure 111

Figure 112

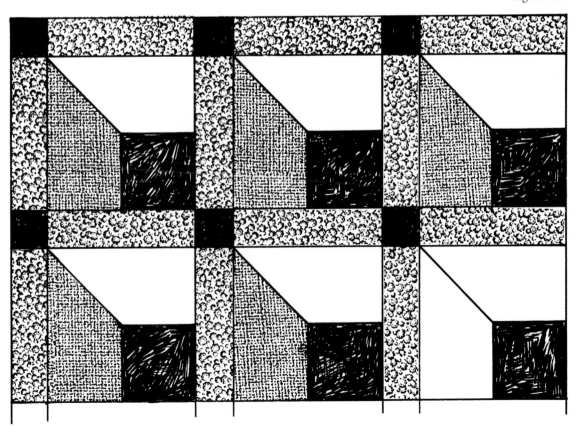

Figure 113

Figure 114

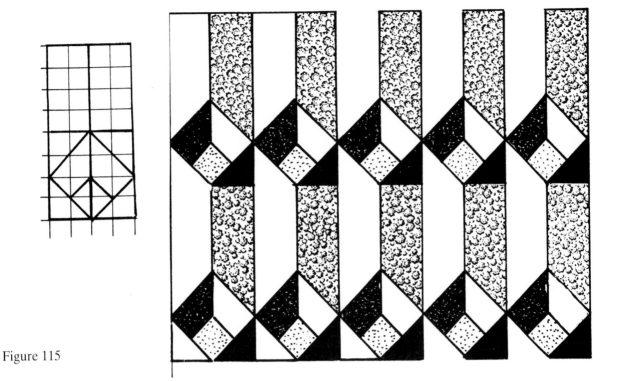

Figure 115

Figure 116

WAISTCOAT (VEST)

When using patchwork as an all-over design on clothes, the patterns of both the patchwork and the garment must be simple. The Santa Maria Formosa floor is a design which would be easy to adapt for use on a simple, semi-fitted waistcoat (see figure 117).

Waistcoat patterns should be chosen very carefully, as this is a garment which can add inches cruelly. If you do not already have a flattering waistcoat pattern in your collection, select one with care and make it up in another fabric before you embark on your patchwork, so that any adjustments can be made to the pattern before you start designing your patchwork.

Make a careful copy of the adjusted pattern on dressmaker's pattern paper having a 10/50 mm grid. Cut the pattern pieces, indicating the seam allowances, as you would cut the cloth, i.e. a left and a right and a complete back. If you have not already done so when adjusting your pattern, allow an extra 13 mm (½ in.) all around if you are going to quilt the garment. Make sure the vertical lines on your grid follow the grain lines of your pattern (figure 118).

If there is a bust dart, draw this in.

Using a backing paper, glue the patterns together on the underarm seam. (A pattern with a curved underarm seam is unsuitable, unless the curve is so slight that it can be straightened without affecting the fit.)

Figure 117

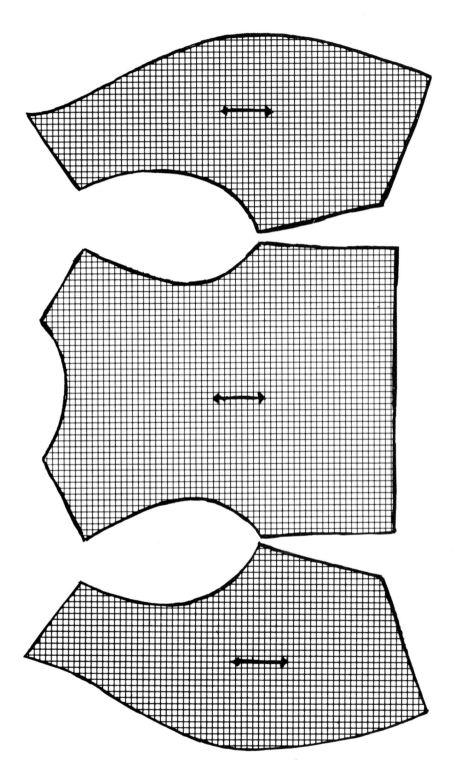

Figure 118

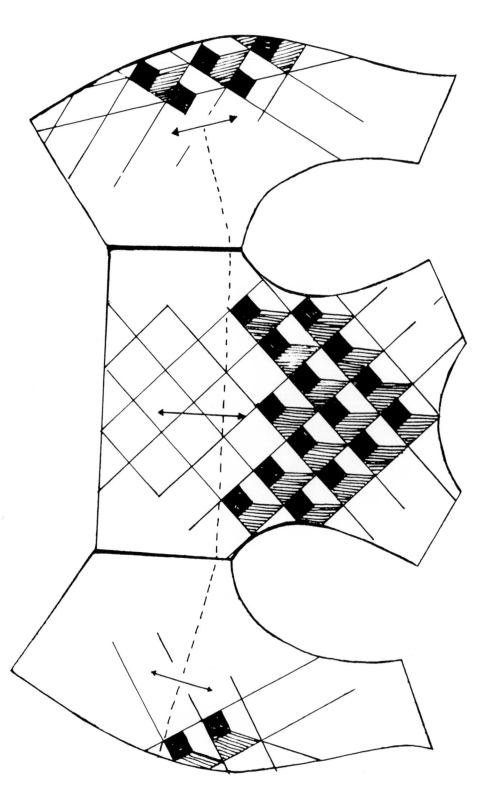

Figure 119

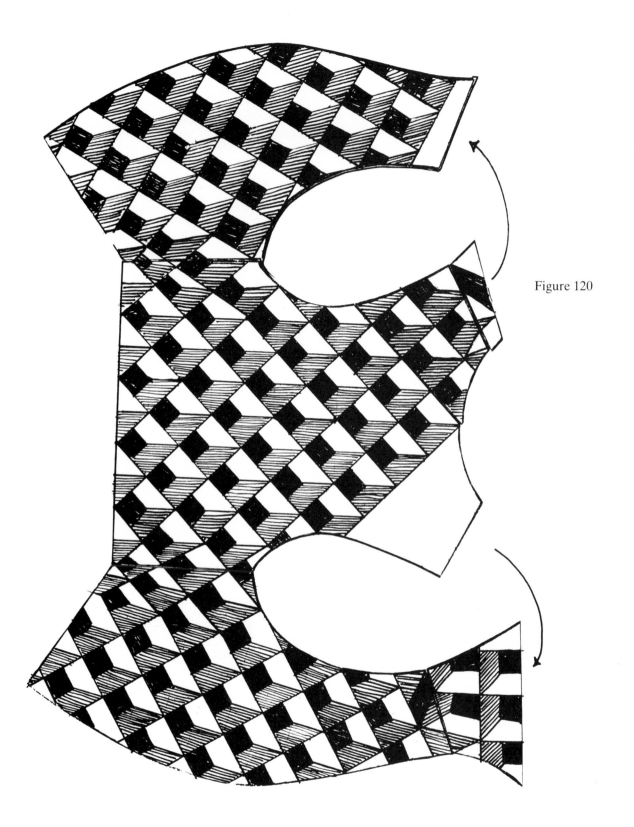

Figure 120

73

Starting at the centre back, draw the patchwork pattern on to the graph paper, leaving the underarm and shoulder areas blank.

Starting at the centre front, draw the patchwork pattern, making sure that the line of the pattern (if any) follows around the garment. If there is a bust dart, leave this area blank (figure 119).

It may be that the back and fronts can be joined without distortion, but experiment with pencil and eraser until you have shapes which are pleasing.

To adjust the templates for the shoulders, pin the shoulder seams together, place over a sleeve board, and alter the pattern until the shapes look pleasant (figure 120).

The bust adjustment is achieved by folding the bust dart together and adapting the templates here (figure 121). There will be some distortion, but the result will still look better than a seamline across the shapes.

There will be no problem cutting pieces for the simple blocks. Graph paper can be used on its own if it is stiff enough, or glued to another paper before being cut out if the graph paper is flimsy. Do not cut papers from the pattern itself.

Underarm, shoulder and bust dart papers should be traced through on to cartridge paper using a ball-point pen, ruler, carbon paper, and a great deal of care to ensure that the tracings are accurate.

The waistcoat illustrated was made from a favourite Vogue pattern which has no bust dart. Figure 122 shows the necessary adaptations to the design.

As each piece is covered, pin the patch to the pattern (it may be necessary to reinforce the paper or pin it to a mounting board). As the patches are joined together they should be pinned back on to the pattern. If this is not done, it is very easy to get confused as to where the adapted blocks should fit in with the normal blocks.

When the patchwork is complete, including the shoulders, and all the papers are removed, press carefully.

The lining should be made up from the original adjusted pattern. If the waistcoat is to be quilted, the patchwork pattern (with underarms joined) is used to cut the wadding, remembering that no seam allowances are required. Tack the shoulders of the wadding together.

The three layers are now fitted together, patchwork on the outside, then wadding, and the lining on the inside. Pin and tack securely in position. Quilt using an embroidery frame, carrying the quilting right up to the edges of the garment.

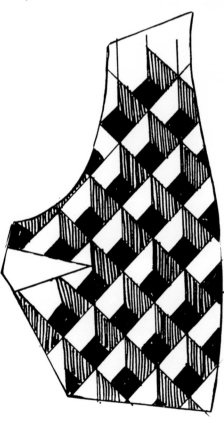

Figure 121

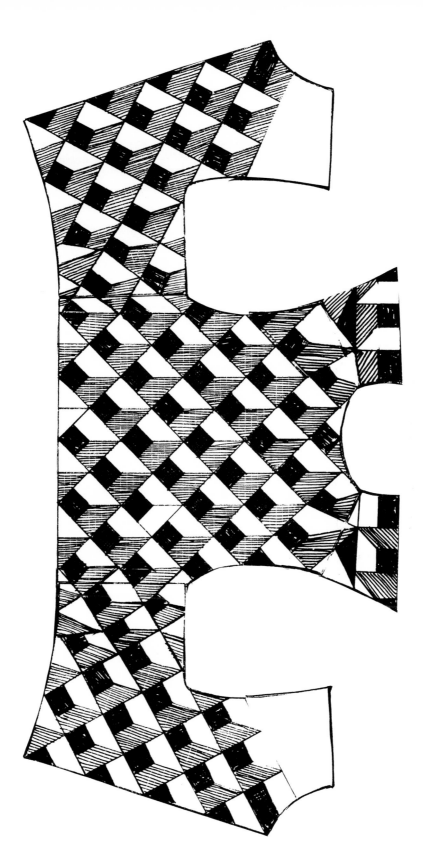

Figure 122

75

FINISHING THE EDGES

There are various ways of finishing the edges of a patchwork waistcoat but the bound edge is quick, neat and effective.

Cut bias strips from one of the fabrics used in the patchwork or from the fabric of the lining. Straighten the edges of the fabric and then measure the same distance from one corner on both the selvedge and the cut end. Using a long ruler, draw lines at right angles from these marks until the cross. Draw a line from the corner through this point. This diagonal line forms a true bias. Make as many additional lines parallel to the first line as there are strips necessary, marking them the required width (figure 123). Cut carefully along the marked lines.

Join the strips by seams that run on the grain of the fabric. Place one strip on top of the other with right sides together and at right angles to each other. Tack and machine along the diagonal. Press the seams open and trim the overlapping points of the strips (figure 124).

The bias strips should be twice the width of the seam allowances to be enclosed, plus turnings on both sides.

Starting at the centre neck, lay the bias strip face down on the right side of the patchwork waistcoat and tack in place, easing the strip around corners by allowing a little extra fullness

Figure 123

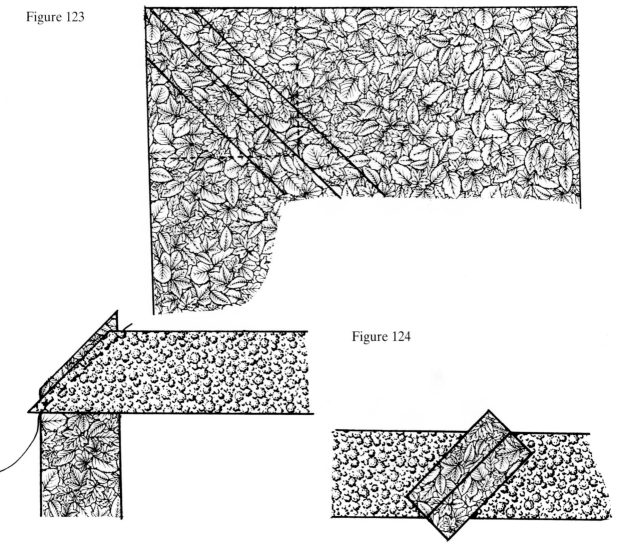

Figure 124

76

(figure 125). When the back of the neck is reached again, fold over the first end of the strip and lay the second end on top of it, so that when the whole is turned over the fold will be outside with no raw edges showing. Hand stitch or machine in the tacked line and remove tacking threads.

Turn the bias so that it encloses the raw edges of the waistcoat, folding under the raw edge of the binding so that it lies along the first seam. Hem the folded edge into the seam (figure 126)

Bind the armholes in the same way.

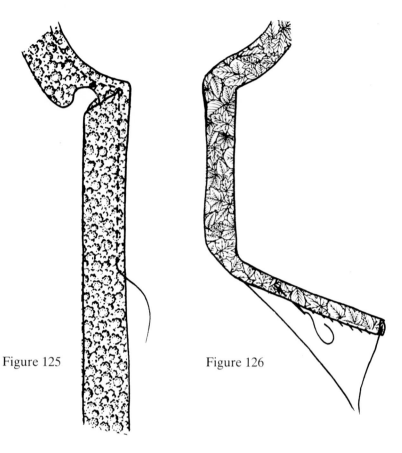

Figure 125

Figure 126

7

St Mark's Floor

MACHINE-MADE QUILT

When you enter St Mark's Basilica from the Piazza San Marco, you will tread a great semi-circle of pavement where nine bands of pattern radiate from the centre steps to a guilloche pattern around the circumference. One of these bands of pattern, in white, grey and black marble, is shown in figure 127. While the edges of the individual blocks are all straight lines, the curve is achieved by varying the dimensions of the sides.

This design lends itself very effectively to quilt-making. The repeat is shown in figure 128.

Templates are the same for both English and American patchwork.

If you are making a quilt for a specific bed, it is best to measure that bed and make the quilt to fit. In this case the quilt was designed and made for a special, King-size, bed and the quilt, without border,

Figure 127

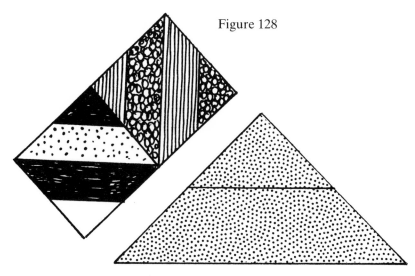

Figure 128

Figure 129

measured 183 cm x 228 cm (72 x 90 in.). The completed square (figure 129) measured approximately 20 cm (8 in.) square. If you are not making a quilt for a specific bed, base your finished size for the quilt on standard sheet sizes.

If the original colour scheme had been followed, the quilt would have been rather drab. Taking into consideration other decoration in the room where it was to go, I substituted brighter colours for the greys and blacks of the floor, but kept the tonal relationships of the original blocks.

The quilt was drawn out to scale, as shown in figure 130, and the templates cut in sandpaper. Fabrics were selected, washed to make sure they did not shrink and the colour did not run, and pressed carefully.

Start in the top left-hand corner and join two half blocks of the repeat shown on p.00 (figure 131). The next row is made up of two full blocks of the repeat and two half blocks (figure 132).

All the rows can be made up singly, but I found it useful to join three rows at a time, working diagonally across the quilt (figure 133).

Cross off the rows on your diagram as you finish them. The feeling of achievement when the longest row, row 10, is completed is quite considerable. If wall space is available, pin the quilt up so progress can be monitored.

Originally it had been intended that a complementary pattern should be used as a border, but when the top was complete, it was decided that to introduce another pattern would make the quilt too fussy. Instead, the quilt was finished with bands of two of the colours used in the blocks.

Because this pattern lends itself to quilting in straight lines, this quilt was quilted by machine. Pinning and tacking the three layers together were done exactly as for the Santa Maria Miracoli quilt in Chapter 5, but with even more care taken to eliminate any possibility of tucks or puckers.

The sewing machine was positioned so that maximum table space was available to the left of the machine – I found the end of the dining table the best place to work. Working on the floor, the quilt was rolled as tightly as possible from the right edge to the middle, and then pinned securely. The roll was introduced under the arm of the machine with the unrolled half of the quilt resting on the table, and the centre line machined from top to bottom.

The roll was then unpinned, opened out to expose a new line for machining, and repinned. This line was then machined from top to bottom. This was repeated until the right side of the quilt was completely machine quilted from top to bottom.

The quilt was then rolled and pinned from the left edge, and machined from bottom to top. Ideally, the lines of machining should alternate from bottom to top and from top to bottom, but on a large quilt this is not possible as it is only just possible to get the half of the quilt, rolled tightly, under the arm of the machine.

When all the vertical lines were machined, the quilt was rolled from the top to the centre and machined from side to side. This complete, it was rolled from the bottom to the centre and the machining completed there as well.

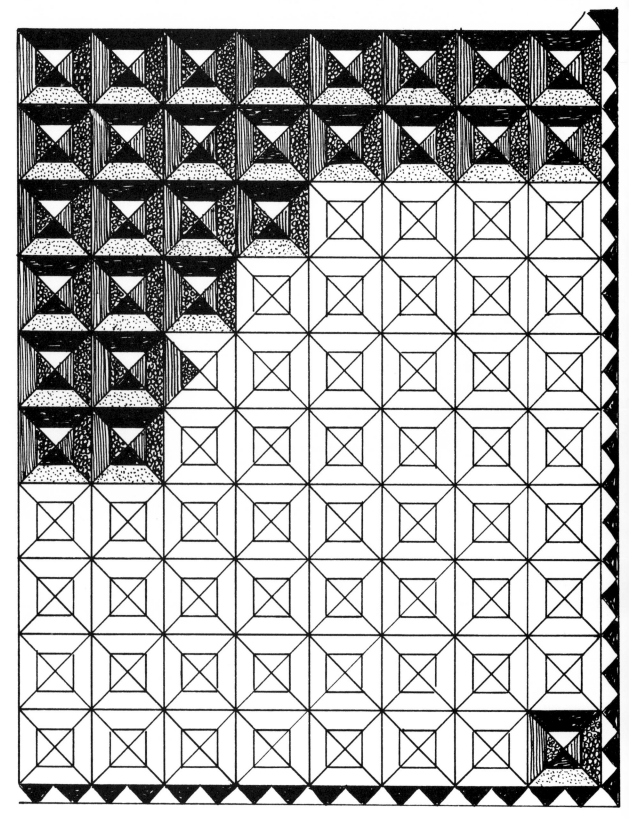

Figure 130

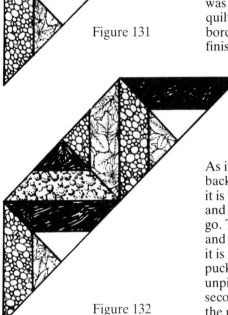

Figure 131

All machining stopped just short of the last border band. The edge was now tacked securely, and the quilt machined all round on the border lines. Mitres were hand finished.

As it is not possible to inspect the back of the quilt as you machine, it is very easy to cause puckers and pleats in the backing as you go. The only remedy is great care, and inspection of each line when it is machined, so that any puckers which occur can be unpicked and resewn before a second line of quilting intensifies the problem.

Figure 132

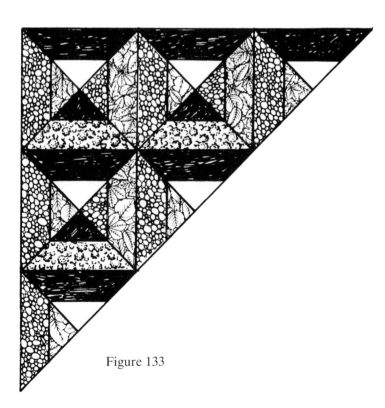

Figure 133

FURTHER DESIGNS

Many of the patterns we found in Venice and Florence can be treated in the same way as this quilt from St Mark's.

The pattern in figures 134 and 135, also from St Mark's, makes up very quickly by machine while the 'quilt' in figure 136, from the atrium of the Basilica, needs only a little more effort than the quilt I made.

Even the quilt corner (figure 137), also from St Mark's, which, at first glance, looks as though it would only be practical made up by the English method, proves quite easy to machine.

Figure 138 shows (a) templates for English patchwork, (b) templates for American patchwork and (c) the American block, which is used both vertically and horizontally to form the repeat.

There is a magnificent floor in San Pietro in Castello (figure 139) which is just another version of the pattern from St Mark's and is worked just as easily by machine.

In time, one comes to recognize the patterns which can easily be adapted. This (figure 140), from St Mark's, seems at first glance to be much too complicated for the American technique, but it is quite straightforward when worked diagonally.

The first Venetian cushion I made was in the pattern shown in figure 141, from the Baptistry at St Mark's. I had made it by hand before I realized that it could have been made up easily by machine if the corners of the outlines of the blocks with square centres were changed as shown in figure 142.

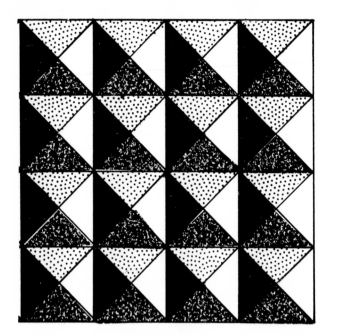

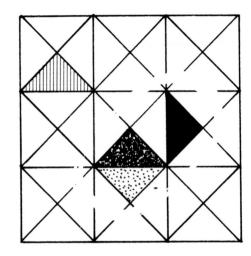

Figure 134

Figure 135

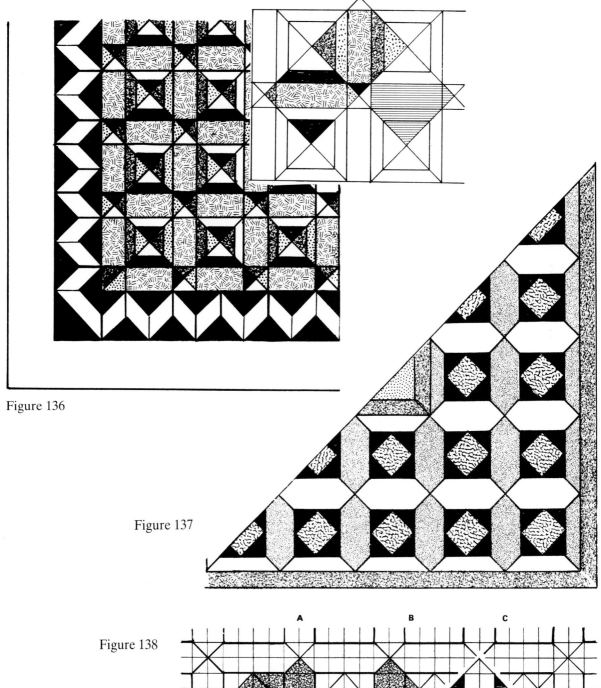

Figure 136

Figure 137

Figure 138

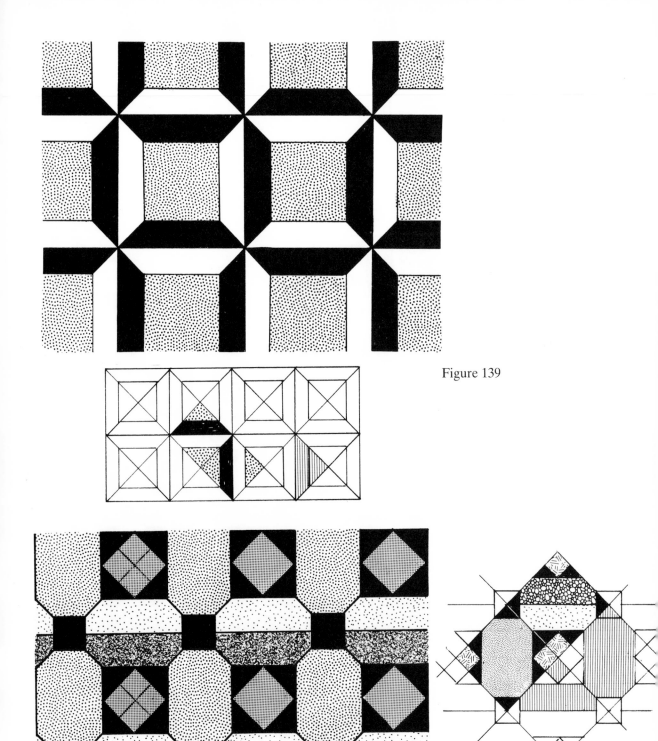

Figure 139

Figure 140

9 Floor pattern from Santa Maria Miracoli. Chapter 5.

10 Mosaic from
SS Maria and Donato,
Murano. Chapter 12.

11 Floor from St Mark
Chapter 1.

12 Cot quilt design from San Francisco del Vigna. Chapter 10.

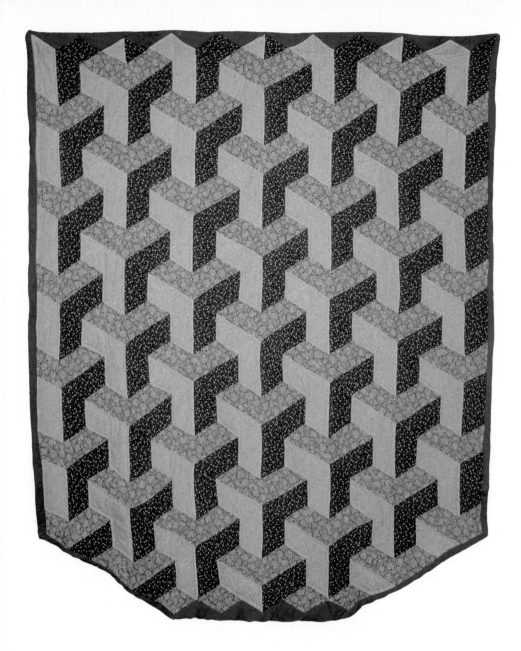

13 Quilt, in American patchwork, using popular trefoil design from St Mark's. Chapter 3.

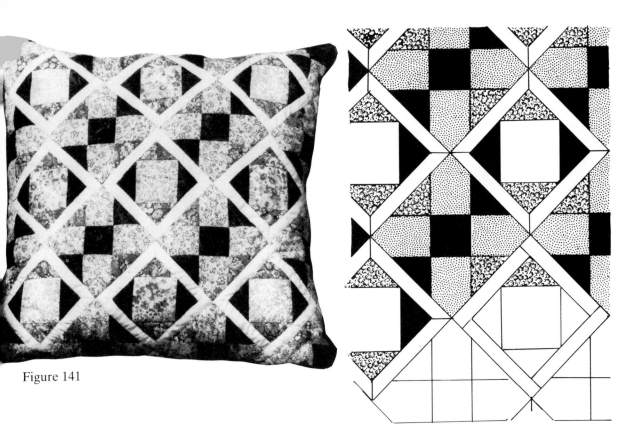

Figure 141

Figure 142

Figure 143

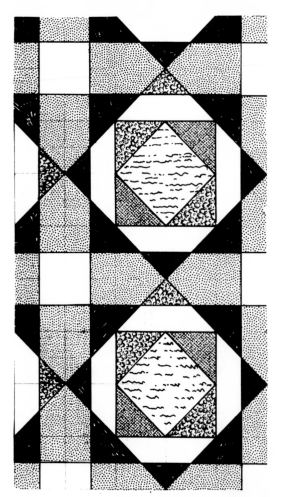

Figure 144

Figure 145

Figure 146

A very similar pattern, found behind the altar in St Mark's, would be simple to make up, using one wide and one narrow diagonal strip alternately (figure 143).

SS Maria and Donato in Murano provided a version without the outline stripe where the diagonal block is obvious (figure 144), while the pattern in figure 145, from St Mark's, simplifies the design still further.

Some patterns lend themselves to being made up either horizontally or diagonally, according to the preference of the maker. The one in figure 146, from St Mark's, is probably easier to work diagonally while figure 147, from the same church, would work equally well either way.

The floor in figure 148, from SS Maria and Donato, would work diagonally as a small block or horizontally as a large one; that shown in figure 149, from St Mark's, would be easier to work diagonally by machine.

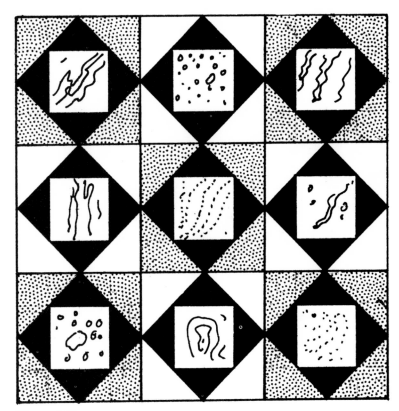

Figure 147

Figure 148

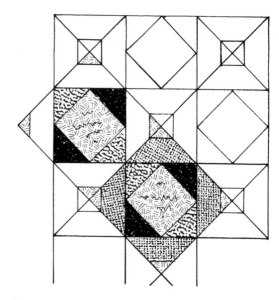

Figure 149

Figure 150

Figure 151

Although the pattern in figure 150 from St Mark's has a strong horizontal pattern line, it could be worked just as easily on the diagonal, as could the pleasantly haphazard pattern in figure 151, from SS Maria and Donato in Murano. Other block patterns have stripes which can be worked equally well horizontally or vertically, as in figures 152, 153 and 154 from St Mark's or figure 155 from SS Maria and Donato in Murano.

Our visit to Florence provided only three patterns in this category, all from the Baptistry of the Duomo. One could be worked either diagonally or horizontally (figure 156), but the other two are vertical patterns (figures 157 and 158).

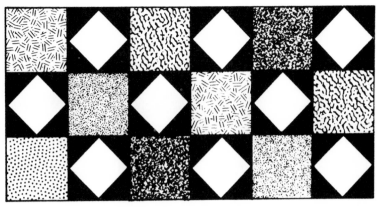

Figure 152

Figure 153

Figure 154

Figure 155

Figure 157

Figure 156

Figure 158

8

Chequerboards

We found two main types of mosaic on Venetian floors. One, usually found on floors dating back to the eleventh century or even earlier, had roughly equal rectangular stone shapes making up patterns or pictures. The other had stones cut in geometrical shapes and fitted closely together to make the kind of patterns seen in earlier chapters in this book.

Sometimes, as in figure 159, the two types were combined.

So far as we could ascertain, none of the floors combining the two techniques was later than the twelfth century. Florentine floors of a similar type were of the same period.

Figure 159

QUILT FROM SAN ZACCARIA (see figures 160 and 161)

My favourite floor of the chequerboard type, incorporating the two styles of mosaic, was found in the Capella di San Tarasio in the Venetian church of San Zaccaria. Here the tiny patterns have been pushed out of shape as the floor heaved

Figure 160

Figure 161

with the floods and earthquakes of eight centuries, but the colour remains bright and glowing.

Although the original mosaic was very tiny, the design does not depend for its effect on scale. I planned a quilt from it which would have the blocks in the second, fourth and sixth rows approx 300 mm (12 in.) square, with the intermediate rows 300 mm (12 in.) wide. The quilt was planned on graph paper. The plan (figure 162) shows rounded corners for the bottom of the quilt, but these could as easily be worked as right angles by repeating the top row.

The blocks were drawn out to scale on graph paper (figure 163) and the templates transferred to sandpaper. Once the dimensions of the 'chequerboard' block were established, instead of cutting a small square, a strip was cut the width of the finished small square and as long as the width of the sandpaper would allow.

The even-numbered rows were worked horizontally by machine. Triangles from the largest template were cut for the odd-numbered rows. It is important to remember that there is a sequence to be followed in putting these together, so I found it useful to pin them into place at the top and bottom of the even-numbered rows until I came to use them (figure 164).

To work the chequerboards, I cut two dark and two light strips of fabric, the width of the small squares of the chequerboards plus turnings. The temptation to tear these strips should be resisted as not all fabrics tear evenly and it will make assembly easier if all the widths are exactly the same.

92

These strips were sewn together, one dark, one light, one dark, one light – making sure that the centre strips were exactly equal in width. These strips of four fabrics were then cut across, making new strips the same width as the original ones. Four of these strips were then sewn together, making sure that the lines were straight and the four central blocks exactly square. The strips are reversed as they are sewn together to get the chequerboard effect (figure 165).

It is necessary to be very careful when machining the original strips together, as a wandering seamline will mean that it is quite impossible to match up the little squares later. It can be useful to mark the sewing lines with the sandpaper template.

Once the required number of chequerboard squares were made up, they were treated as units in the design and the odd rows

Figure 162

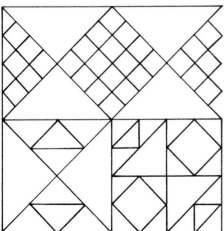

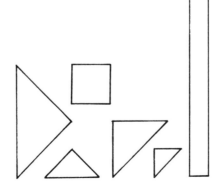

Figure 163

93

Figure 164

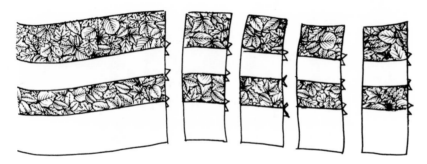

Figure 165

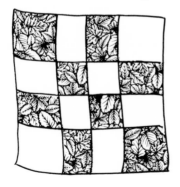

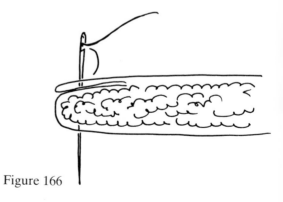

Figure 166

worked horizontally across the quilt by adding the triangles already cut. The strips were then joined together to make the quilt top.

A border was added to finish the quilt, and then the backing was laid out on the carpet, the wadding was spread on top of that, and the patchwork on top, right side up. This time the backing, wadding and top were all the same size.

When the three thicknesses were pinned and tacked together, the raw edges of both the backing and the patchwork were turned in and tacked together, enclosing the wadding, the extra width of which was rolled to make a firm edge (figure 166).

USING A QUILTING FRAME

There are several types of quilting frame available. The one we had when I was a child was simplicity itself. The runners were two lengths of 50 x 25 mm (2 x 1 in.) planed wood. These were clamped on to two shorter pieces of the same wood (figure 167), and the frame was supported on the backs of chairs. When the quilting was finished for the day, the frame was unclamped, rolled up, and stored out of the way. Quilting was done in the living-room when the light was good during the day, the men were out at work, and the children at school.

Commercial frames are available which use a more sophisticated version of the same principle.

To set the quilt up for quilting in a frame, one side should be stitched to the canvas covering the side runner. The quilt is then wound around this runner until only about 600 mm (24 in.) is left free, and this side is stitched to the canvas on the other runner. The runners are then fixed between the stretchers and adjustments made until the quilt is held firmly between the runners, top side up (figure 168). Tapes are then pinned in place over the stretchers to hold the exposed part of the quilt taut.

As the exposed length of the quilt is worked, the tape is removed from the stretchers, the runners loosened and then turned so that the next area is exposed. The runners are then retightened, the tapes replaced, and the quilting recommenced. When the quilt is complete, it is taken off the

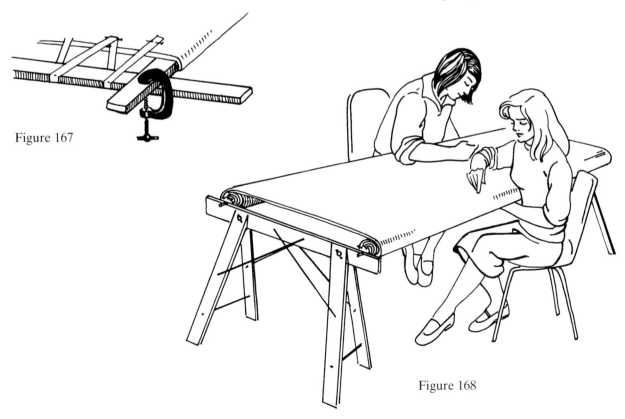

Figure 167

Figure 168

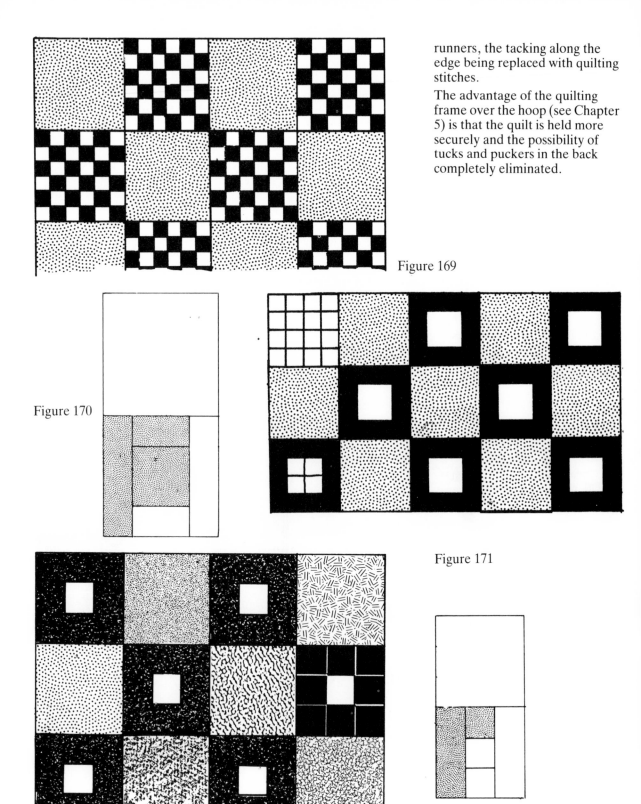

runners, the tacking along the edge being replaced with quilting stitches.

The advantage of the quilting frame over the hoop (see Chapter 5) is that the quilt is held more securely and the possibility of tucks and puckers in the back completely eliminated.

Figure 169

Figure 170

Figure 171

FURTHER DESIGNS

There are a number of other patterns of the 'chequerboard' family which can easily be worked by machine, the one shown in figure 169, from St Mark's, being an obvious example. Two other similar patterns (figure 170) were made up of small squares in the original floors. They could be worked just as well with the templates shown (figure 171) unless the effect of the texture of patchwork squares was desired.

Some of the most effective chequerboard patterns, however, are much more likely to be successful if worked in the English technique. The first, like

Figure 172

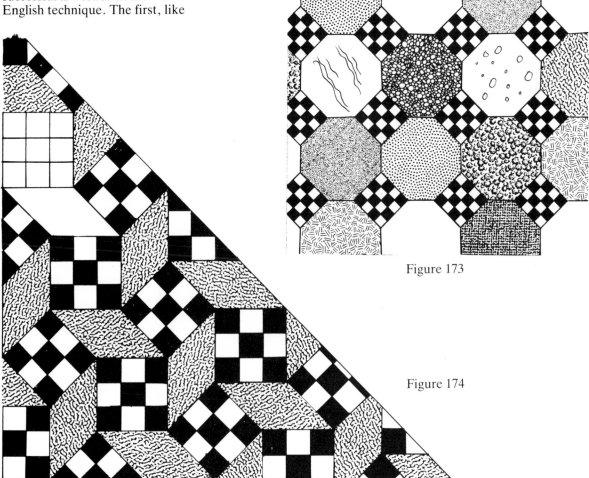

Figure 173

Figure 174

the quilt, from San Zaccaria, was set on the diagonal on the original floor (figure 172).

The two shown in figures 173 and 174, from St Mark's, are much too complicated to be worked by machine or even by hand in the American technique.

Florence provided no new versions of the chequerboard, though several designs found in the Baptistry could be worked with the strip technique. One, a pattern of red, black, and cream (figure 175), could almost be a weaving pattern, while in figure 176 the strips are made up in the usual way, but then cut and joined at an angle of 60° to make a chevron pattern. The third design (figure 177) combines the two techniques most effectively.

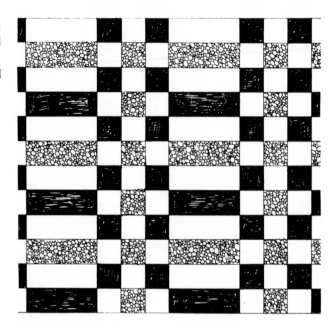

Figure 175

Figure 176

Figure 177

98

9
Medallions & Borders

MEDALLIONS

Almost every Venetian church
we visited had, in doorways or on
altar steps, designs which could
be used for medallions in the
centres of quilts, or for cushions
or wall hangings. The design in
figure 178 is a somewhat
simplified version of a floor in St
Mark's Cathedral.

WALL-HANGING FROM
UCCELLO'S DOORSTEP

The medallion I fell in love with
is from the floor of the left
doorway into St Mark's. There is
a story that the pattern was
designed by Paolo Uccello (1397-
1475). It is recorded that he
designed some of the ceiling
mosaics in St Mark's so it is quite
possible that this is also his, as he
was fascinated by geometric
problems, and this floor is quite
unlike any other in the Basilica.

I chose to make the design into a
wall-hanging (figure 179) and, in
order to reproduce the glowing
colour, to work in Thai silk using
the English technique. On the
original floor the design in the
corner of the square was laid in
small mosiac stones in the

Figure 178

Figure 179

When the circle pieces had been joined together, the corner pieces were worked. A medium-weight Vilene[1] was covered first with grey silk and then a layer of black, the black being big enough to be stitched over to the back of the Vilene. The Vilene was used instead of paper as a shape, but left in when the work was done.

The scroll pattern was then traced from the lining paper on to greaseproof paper, and the outlines pricked with a needle to create tiny holes all the way along the lines. (If the needle is set in a cork, see figure 180, the work is made easier.)

The pricked paper was laid on the black silk shape and pinned in position with fine needles. Talcum powder was 'pounced' through the holes with a pad of rolled-up felt. The paper pattern was then lifted off very carefully and the lines were traced with a fine brush and white watercolour.

The layers were then tacked together, avoiding the motif to be worked, with rows of fairly bold tacking stitches.

Working a little at a time (because of the fraying properties of the silk) the centre of the stems and leaves were cut through the black silk only, the edges folded

[1] American readers: nonwoven interfacing

technique known as Opus Vermiculatum – where patterns are built up with curving lines of changing colours.

It seemed to me that this effect could be achieved by using San Blas appliqué (the method used by the Panamanian Indians to decorate their clothing).

The whole design was drawn up, full size, on lining paper, using compass and ruler and following sketches and photographs of the original as closely as possible. Grain lines were marked on each individual piece.

The whole of the central circle was then traced on to cartridge paper, grain lines included. The lining paper pattern was then pinned to a display board, and, as each piece of cartridge paper was covered with silk, it was pinned into place on this pattern. Fine needles were used in place of pins to fasten the pieces in place, as pins would have marked the silk. All joining was done with silk sewing threads because of the delicacy of the fabric.

A word of warning to anyone who attempts working patchwork with Thai silk: as well as being extremely expensive, Thai silk has to be cut with generous turnings as it frays at the slightest touch. It is not easy to work with, but the colour and texture make the extra effort worthwhile.

Figure 180

100

under and stitched down (figure 181). For ease of explanation the colours are reversed in the diagram.

Great care was taken when turning the silk under. The fold had to be exactly on the white line, and the hemming done with black silk thread. Corners, where no material could be turned under, needed neatening with buttonhole stitch to give a firm edge. The other three corners were worked in the same manner.

The outside border pieces were also tacked over Vilene, and attached to the curved sections, the whole being joined together to make the complete pattern.

A backing was made of heavy silk, and a circle of light, 50 gm (2 oz.) wadding laid in position on it, directly under the centre of the pattern. All papers were removed but the Vilene kept in position, and the main shapes of the polyhedron were quilted, as were the circles, and the outside square.

The edge was finished with a piping of black silk, and a tube made along the top of the back for a piece of finished wood to be inserted to hold the hanging flat and in position. To this tube, plastic curtain rings were stitched as hangers (figure 182).

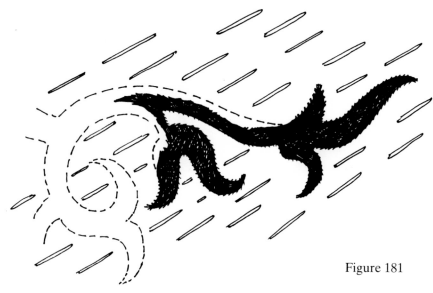

Figure 181

BORDERS

If it is desired to use any of these medallions as the centres for quilts, it will be necessary to build up the shape with a border or borders. This, then, seems to be a good place to include those we collected.

In St Mark's the commonest border is the plain length of cut stone, generally in a pale cream or grey, with corners often neatly mitred. These outline patterns divide one pattern from another, and one area of floor from another.

Other 'floors' are outlined by two rows of pale stone strips with a row of hexagons between them (figure 183). In some places we found double rows of shapes used as outlines (figures 184, 185 and 186), whilst in others, patterns which elsewhere were used as all-over patterns, were used as borders (figures 187, 188, 189, 190, 191, 192 and 193).

Later churches and scuolae in Venice had borders which were possibly more useful to us (figures 194, 195 and 196 from the Scuola San Rocco), but the ultimate in stone borders comes from the curious church of Orsanmichele in Florence (Figure 197).

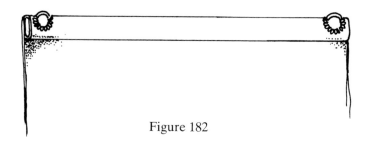

Figure 182

101

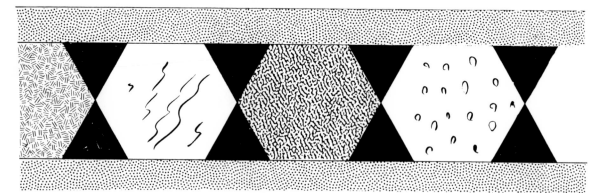

Figure 183

Figure 184

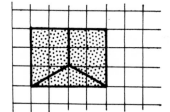

Figure 185

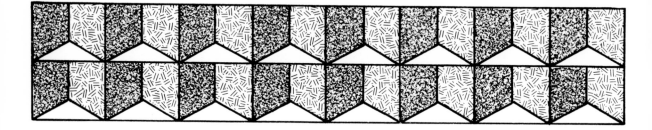

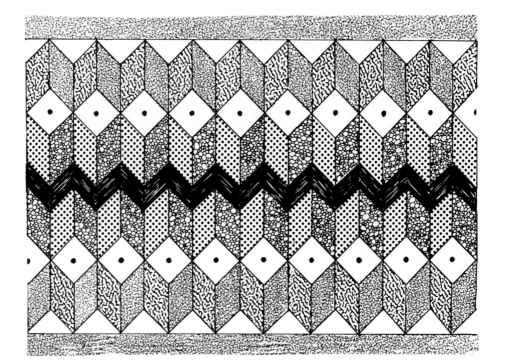

Figure 186

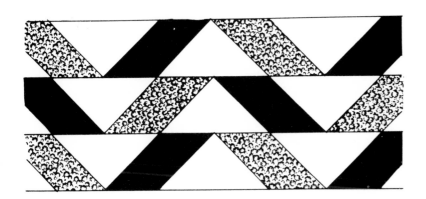

Figure 187

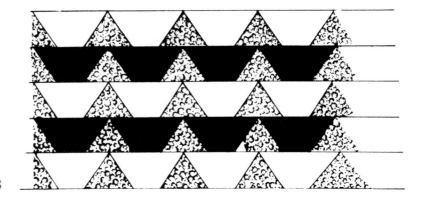

Figure 188

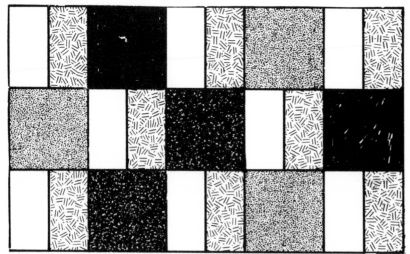

Figure 189

Figure 190

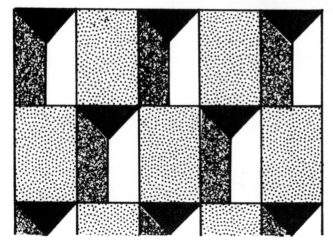

Figure 191

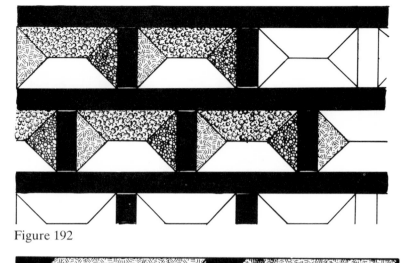

Figure 192

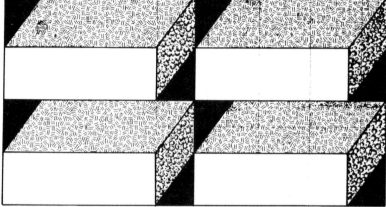

Figure 193

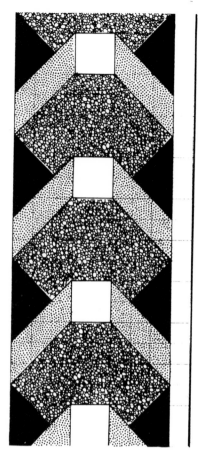

Figure 196

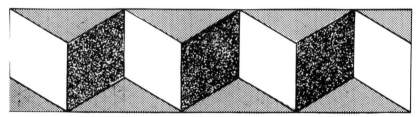

Figure 194

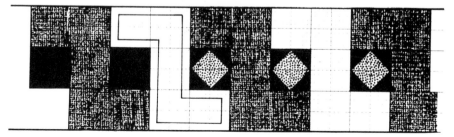

Figure 195

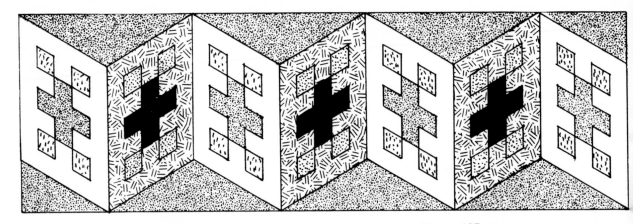

Figure 197

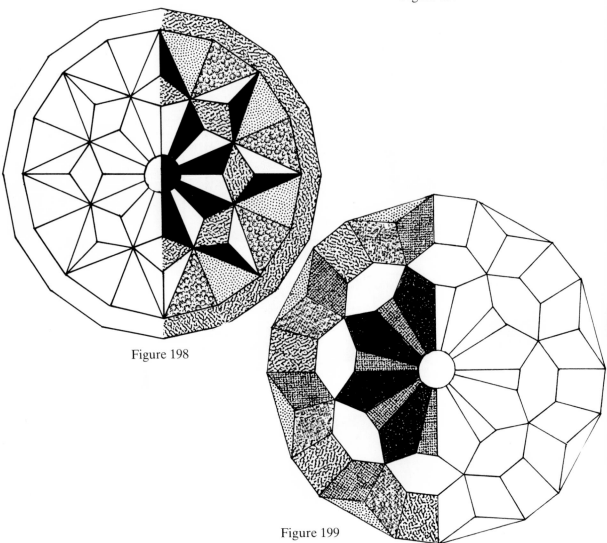

Figure 198

Figure 199

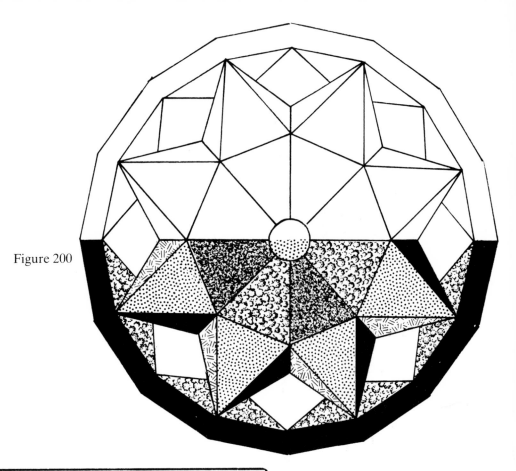

Figure 200

FURTHER MEDALLIONS & BORDERS

Venice yielded numbers of these patterns, some of them circular and promising use as cushions, or the centres for medallion quilts. These three patterns (figures 198, 199 and 200) come from the magnificent floors of the Scuola San Rocco, while the circle within a square in figure 201 came from the great church of SS Giovanni and Paolo.

Figure 201

Figure 202

Border
repeat

We found medallions with their own elaborate borders, like figure 202 from San Niccolo di Tolentini, or figure 203 from San Giorgio Maggiore; and a version of this design, with a different centre, in SS Giovanni and Paolo (figure 204).

Centres were obviously a problem for the paviors. It is just as difficult for patchworkers to achieve a really neat centre when joining more than six or eight pieces. The paviors got around the problem by making a centre circle, and so can we. If a large circle is wanted it can be applied after the pieces are joined (figure 205) or a small circle can be achieved (and an untidy join concealed) by embroidering a centre with the ribbed or backstitched spider's web (figure 206).

Figure 203

Figure 204

Figure 205

Figure 206

Figure 207

San Giorgio Maggiore provided us with a simpler version of the star in a square (figure 207), and San Pietro in Castello a simpler form still (figure 208).

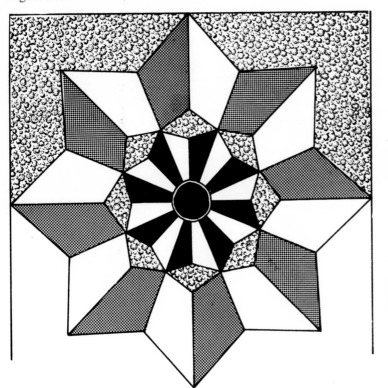

Figure 208

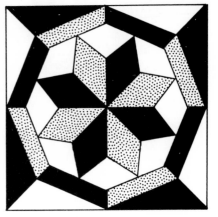

Figure 209

The altar steps in San Giorgio
Maggiore had patterns based on
the square and on rectangles
(figures 209, 210 and 211), and
we found one pattern, from a
glorious floor in the Scuola San
Rocco in Venice, which could
almost make a quilt in itself
(figure 212).

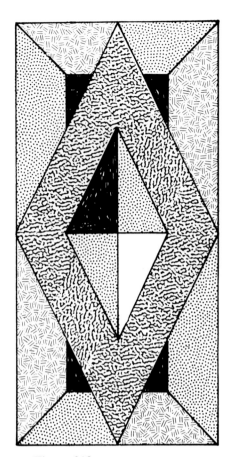

Figure 210

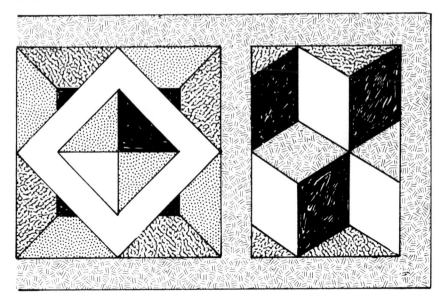

Figure 211

111

Figure 212

Florence, curiously, yielded no patterns of this type, the churches of the period being more concerned with painted decoration. In the little church of San Miniato al Monte high above the Arno we did find a little wall decoration in black and white marble (figure 213) which would make a very effective cushion.

Figure 213

112

10

Hexagonal Blocks & Eight-Pointed Stars

The hexagonal blocks found in the outer circle of Uccello's doorstep (figure 214) formed a favourite pattern with Venetian paviors. It appears in various forms, but most often with a little connecting post separating the rows, allowing one to look down on to the flattened hexagon which makes the top of the figure.

EVENING BAG

Two versions of this form (figures 215 and 216) from St Mark's floors were used for the two sides of an evening bag. The material used was navy blue silk shantung, with scraps of figured Thai silk I had been hoarding for years. Accents were picked out in the white silk used for lining.

Because the scale makes really fine detail difficult to achieve, the pegs on the front panel were applied to the tops of the hexagons, the raw edges of the ends being covered when the two blocks were sewn together (figure 217). For the same reason, the black accents on the bar between the octagonal blocks on the back panel were omitted.

The patchwork for the bag was planned on graph paper, and the patchwork panels made up by the English method.

A strip of shantung, finished width 50 mm (2 in.), was stitched between the two sections of patchwork, as shown in figure 218. Further strips 100 mm (4 in.) wide were stitched at the top ends of the bag, and some 75 mm (3 in.) wide were added along the length of both sides. The

patchwork areas were approximately 145 x 215 mm (5¾ x 8½ in.).

Using a backing of calico, and 50 gm. (2 oz.) wadding, the outlines of the octagons were quilted. A row of quilting was then worked down both sides 7 mm (¼ in.) from the patchwork design, continuing around the top ends 12 mm (½ in.) from the patchwork.

Figure 214

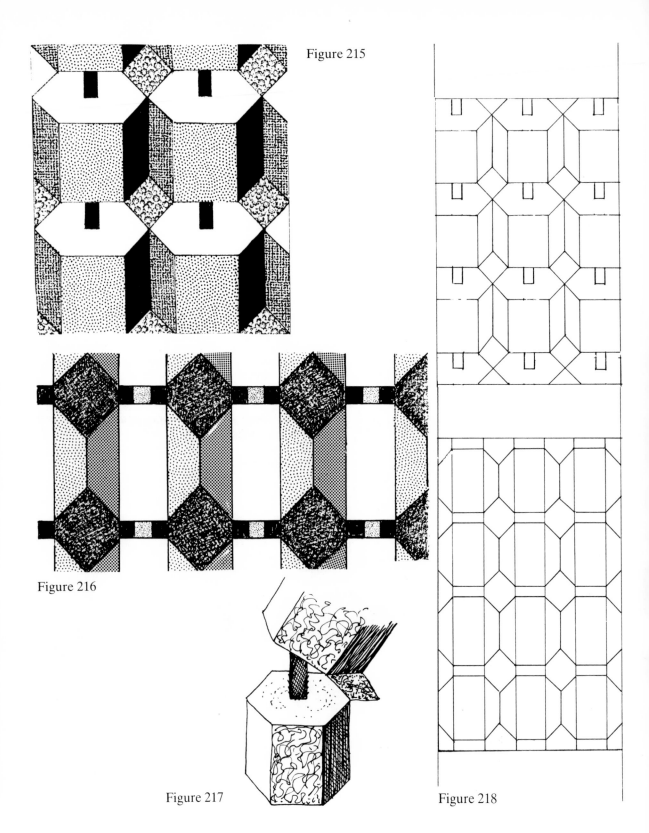

Figure 215

Figure 216

Figure 217

Figure 218

The side edges were carefully folded under 7 mm (¼ in.) from the first line of quilting, and stitched through all the thicknesses of the materials. The wadding was then trimmed off to this line. The two edges were turned in 40 mm (1½ in.) from the top of the patchwork design and stitched through all thicknesses of fabric.

The whole article was folded in half along the bottom piece of the bag, right sides together, matching up the top edges of the two patchwork panels. The sides were then stitched together, through the silk and the calico, making a gusset 25 mm (1 in.) deep to level with the top of the patchwork panels (figure 219). The bag was then turned right side out (figure 220).

A zip fastener was attached to the top 40 mm (1½ in.) from the stitched fold at the top of the bag. When the zip was in place, stitched to both sides of the bag, the tops were folded down and stitched through all thicknesses along the line originally quilted 12 mm (½ in.) from the top of the patchwork panels.

Three bias strips about 600 mm (24 in.) long and 50 mm (2 in.) wide were cut in blue silk and stitched into three tubes which were turned out, enclosing the

seams. The ends of these three tubes were stitched together and secured, and then the three were plaited together carefully to form a handle for the bag. The second end was stitched securely together when the plait was completed.

The ends of the plait were slipped between the zip and the gussets at each side of the bag and stitched in place. The tops of the gussets were neatened by folding in the raw edges and stitching them together at each side.

Figure 221

Figure 219

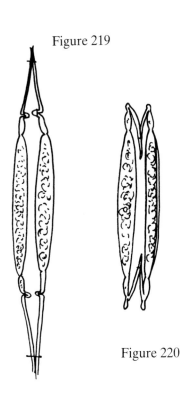

Figure 220

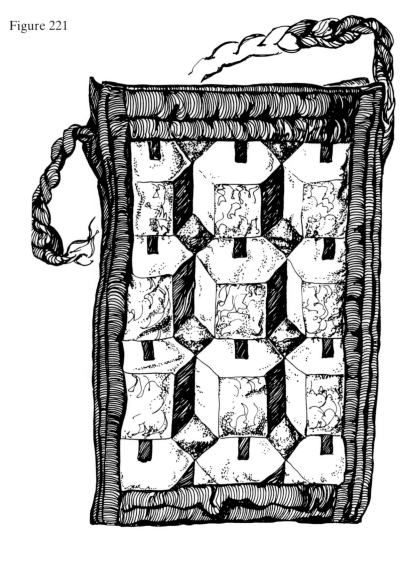

115

A bag of white silk was made to fit, and slid into place for a lining. The folded-over top edge was stitched into position on the inside of the zip fastener, far enough from the teeth that the material would not catch in use. Figure 221 shows the front of the bag, and figure 222 the reverse.

FURTHER DESIGNS

We found a variation on the hexagon and post design in the church of San Pietro in Castello, (figure 223), whilst in the church of Madonna del Orto, the shape was so distorted as to be hardly recognizable (figure 224). If this version were used for patchwork, I should be inclined to embroider the post.

There is a very complicated pattern in St Mark's which could be described as octagons within octagons (figure 225). The design comes from one of the oldest floors in St Mark's, and I was so charmed by it that I made a cushion from it (see figure 226). Unfortunately, at that scale the pattern is so busy it is difficult to make sense of it, and I feel that the result was something less than a success.

The design could also be considered a variation on the eight-pointed star mentioned in the introduction, several variations of which we found in Venice. That shown in figure 227, with a boxed centre, was found in Santa Maria della Salute, whilst a similar version was found in the church of San Francisco del Vigna. This I found so attractive I made it up into a cot quilt for a small nephew (figure 228).

Our search in Florentine churches produced only one eight-pointed star floor (in the Baptistry of the Duomo) – a pattern which also appears in the Roman floor discovered at Fishbourne in Sussex (figure 229) – and a contemporary painted border in the Sacristy of San Miniato al Monte carried the design even further (figure 230).

The mosaic in the background of a niche holding a statue at the doorway of the Duomo in Florence had this glittering mosaic in red and gold, blue and white (figure 231).

Figure 222

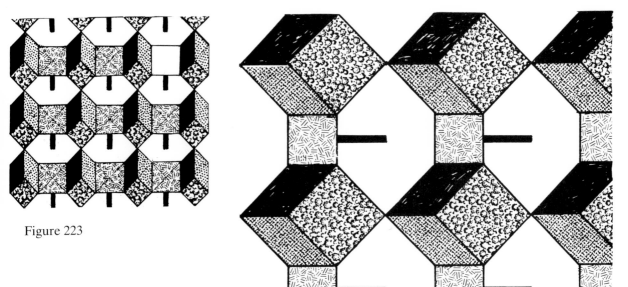

Figure 223

Figure 224

Figure 225

Figure 226

Figure 227

Figure 228

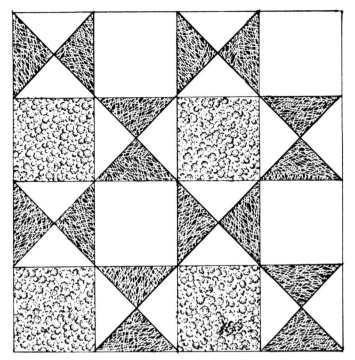

Figure 229

Figure 230

Figure 231

119

11

Curved Blocks & All-Over Patterns

EXAMPLES FROM VENICE AND FLORENCE

On the first visit to Venice I dismissed all patterns with curved blocks as being too difficult to come within the scope of this book, but on the subsequent visit, and even more on a trip to Florence, I realized that to leave these out would be to ignore some very valuable material. The pattern in figure 232 comes from one of the oldest floors in St Mark's, and the black filling is made up of tiny chips of black marble.

The pattern shown in figure 233 (an early inspiration for clamshell patchwork?) is one of the curved segments radiating from the central steps in the atrium of St Mark's, while figure 234, from the Baptistry of St Mark's, is based on isometric projection.

It was in Florence, however, that the really glorious floors were found. In San Miniato al Monte we found the panel in figures 235 and 236, with a block reminiscent of the American patchwork block, 'Drunkard's Path', while in the Baptistry of the Duomo we found a further complication of the same idea (figures 237 and 238).

JOINING CURVED SEAMS

Great care and very accurate joining of the patches is required when making up a pattern with curved seams (figure 239). In the English technique the papers are covered in the usual manner, but the fabric needs to be eased very carefully on the inside curves. It may be necessary to make nicks in the edge of the fabric, but these should not be deep enough to reach the edge of the paper, as this would weaken the edge to be sewn.

To join curved patches I find it best to start at the centre of a curve and work to each end

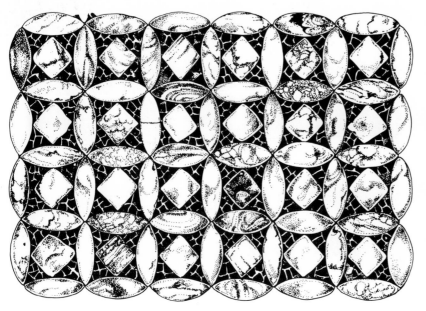

Figure 232

Figure 233

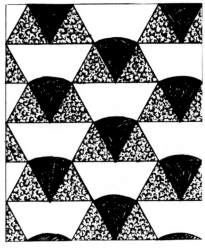

Figure 234

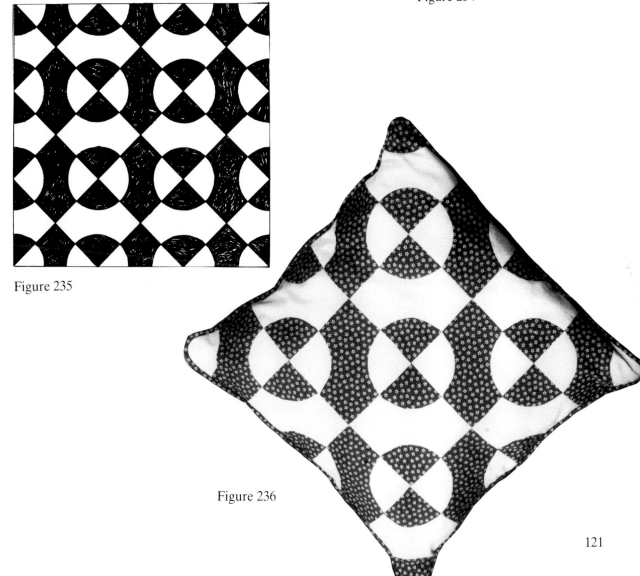

Figure 235

Figure 236

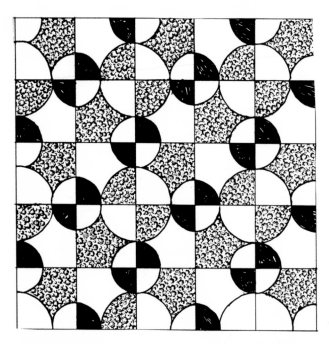

Figure 237

Figure 238

Figure 239

Figure 240

Figure 241

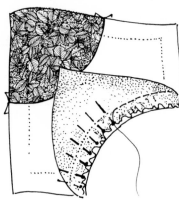

Figure 242

(figure 240), making sure that the curve is eased carefully so that the patches do not overlap at the end (figure 241). Sometimes a pin will help.

Patchwork with curved blocks can be worked by machine, and some will find it easier to work curved seams by the American method by hand than to do it with papers in the English fashion. Seamlines should be clearly marked and pinned, with running stitches or backstitches worked on the marked lines, making sure that each stitch goes through the lines on both pieces of fabric (figure 242).

I worked cushions in the circle patterns from San Miniato al Monte and the Baptistry and found that, while it was more exacting than working patchwork on straight lines, the result justified the extra effort. The second pattern was particularly difficult, the problem being to ensure that the straight lines matched up to make the series of squares.

The Baptistry provided other designs with curves, one being a version of the eight-pointed star design (figure 243), whilst a second decorated the tilted squares surrounding a cross (figure 244), and a third combined a 'Drunkard's Path' block with strips (figure 245). A further eye-dazzling pattern from the Baptistry in Florence, dating from the twelfth century (figure 246) echoes an even older one from St Mark's (figure 247).

We found one curved pattern in the Baptistry in Florence which I am sure could be worked in patchwork, but I do not care to attempt it myself (figure 248).

The oldest floors in Venice have some patterns so complicated that they would be very difficult

Figure 243

Figure 244

Figure 245

Figure 246

123

Figure 247

Figure 248

to work other than by English patchwork. The one shown in figure 249 makes a very lovely black and silver pattern on the floor near the entrance from the Piazetta dei Leoncini, and the windmill in figures 250 and 251, also from St Mark's, is one we have already met in the chapter on chequerboard patterns.

Figure 249

Figure 250

Figure 251

Figure 252

Several versions of the boxed cross pattern in figure 252 were found in St Mark's and in SS Maria and Donato in Murano, while another cross pattern, from St Mark's, is superimposed on the common long hexagon design from Chapter 1 (figure 253).

Another cross pattern, also from St Mark's, could, with adaptation of the templates (dividing the lozenge in one row and the triangle in the other), be made up by machine as a strip pattern (figure 254).

I found the windmill pattern particularly attractive and made it up into a cushion, trimmed with a piped edge.

Figure 253

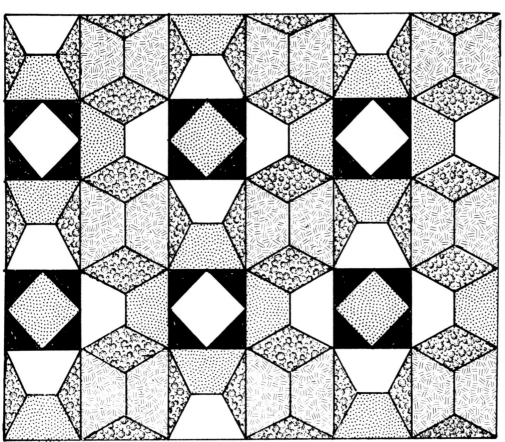

Figure 254

PIPED EDGES

Piping makes a very attractive edging for many articles, not just cushions or hangings, and many people worry that it is too difficult for a beginner to attempt. With care this should not be so.

Piping is a cord, covered with a strip of material into which it is sewn. Soft white cord may be purchased specially for this purpose, or a fine cord or woollen thread used, depending on the effect required. This cord should be washed before use to insure against shrinkage when the article is made up.

The strip of fabric, cut on the cross as shown in Chapter 6, is folded over the piping cord and secured in place by running stitches set close up against the cord (figure 255).

The piping cord is placed on the right side of the patchwork and attached by running stitches (or machine stitches using a zip foot) through all three thicknesses, care being taken to stitch close to the cord as before (figure 256).

The backing material is then placed face down on to the piping, and attached with running or machine stitches in the same way, again making sure to stitch close to the cord (Figure 257).

Corners may present difficulties. Too sharp a corner, even though carefully snicked (figure 258), may stick out in a dog-ear when the cushion is stuffed, so, if the pattern allows, the corner should be slightly rounded (figure 259). When turned out to the right side, the piping should present a firm edging to the cushion and no stitching should show.

Figure 255

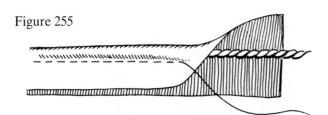

Figure 256

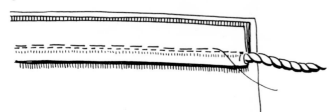

Figure 257

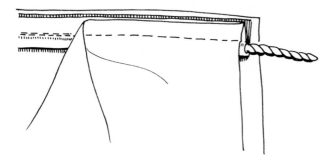

Figure 258

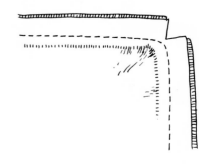

Figure 259

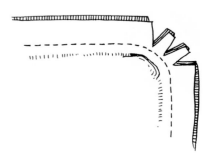

12
Quilts

STONE QUILTS FROM ST MARK'S AND SS MARIA AND DONATO

While any of the patterns shown in the preceding chapters could be made up into quilts, either on their own or in combination with others, in St Mark's Basilica and in the ancient church of SS Maria and Donato we found sections of the floors laid in such a way that a pattern could be taken exactly as it was found, enlarged (for the most part the 'quilts' in St Mark's are less than 60 cm (2 ft) square), and made up, borders and all, into very useful square quilts.

Figure 260

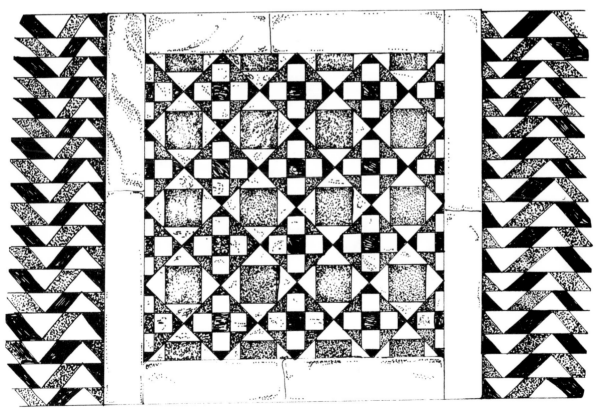

The quilts heading Chapters 1 and 9 were found in St Mark's, as were the two in figures 261 and 262. The square centre motifs of these quilts would be difficult to change to adapt them to a normal bed shape, but it would be very easy to adjust the rows of pattern at the sides and top and bottom to achieve the required proportions.

Some patterns we found can be used almost unchanged, except for scaling up of size, since the pavior laid them in oblong shapes. Just inside the main door of St Mark's (which is usually used only for ceremonial occasions) is the splendid pattern in Figure 263, almost quilt-sized, in soft shades of blue and golden marbles.

Figure 261

Figure 262

In SS Maria and Donato there are several patterns which are oblong, and which would make very attractive quilts with no basic change of shape (figures 264, 265 and 266). One pattern from Murano (figure 267) was not quite a quilt, being an infill at the edge of a floor, but it could easily be adapted to quilt proportions by extending the lattice border another row or two.

As all the methods necessary for making up any of these quilts have been described in full in other chapters, I will not include them here.

I liked the St Mark's floor in figure 268 so much that I made it up by machine as a wall hanging, though it could as easily have been used as a cot quilt.

Figure 263

Figure 264

Figure 265

Figure 266

Figure 267

Figure 268

FURTHER DESIGNS

Any reader who visits Venice or Florence with an open eye will doubtless find patterns we missed. Other cities in Italy are certain to provide more patterns – Rome and Ravenna in particular. I am told that the Greek islands and Yugoslav harbours, which were once part of the Venetian Empire, can show floors to rival those in Venice.

It is, of course, possible to seek out these patterns secondhand. In the National Gallery in London there is a 'Madonna and Child Enthroned' painted by Giovanni Bellini where a splendid floor is faithfully reproduced (figure 269).

When, in the thirteenth century, Henry III's tomb in Westminster Abbey was being decorated, a mosaic master was summoned from Italy. Tantalizing fragments of his work still remain (figures 270 and 271).

Quite a number of great houses in England have floors in wood or marble which were obviously inspired by Italian mosaic floors. Ham House has the floor shown in figure 272 in coloured woods, while that shown in figure 273 comes from Apsley House, the home of the Duke of Wellington.

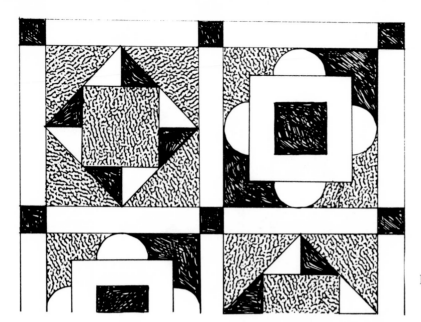

Figure 269

Figure 270

138

Figure 271

Figure 272

Towards the end of the last century, and into the first decade of this one, many much humbler homes had their floors decorated with patchwork patterns in ceramic tiles. Figure 274 is from the hall of a late Victorian house in Crouch Street, Banbury, in Oxfordshire.

Many churches of the late Victorian period and of the first decade of this century had floors lavishly decorated with ceramic tiles based on these or similar patterns. Some museums, with comprehensive collections of twelfth- to fourteenth-century architecture, have items which could serve as source material.

Once your eye has been trained to see patchwork patterns, you will find they turn up everywhere. I hope you will gain as much enjoyment as I have from seeking them out and turning them into fabric designs.

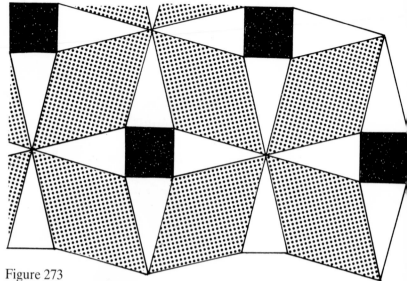

Figure 273

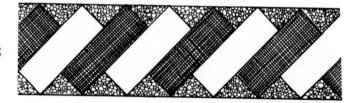

Figure 274

Suppliers Of Patchwork Materials & Equipment

U.K.

The Patchwork Dog and the
Calico Cat,
21 Chalk Farm Road,
Chalk Farm,
London, N.W.1

Village Fabrics,
Dept. EM,
44 Braywick Road,
Maidenhead, Berks SL6 1DA

Pioneer Patches,
Inglewood Lodge,
Birkby Road,
Huddersfield,
West Yorkshire, HD2 2DA

John Lewis Partnership,
Oxford Street and Brent Cross,
London.
Milton Keynes.
Peter Jones, Sloane St, London
& Trewins, Watford

Magpie,
621 Wimbourne Road,
Winton,
Bournemouth,
Dorset, BH9 2AR

U.S.A.

Batting and Pillow Forms

Fairfield Processing Corporation
P.O. Box 1130
Danbury, CT 06810
Polyfil®, Extra-Loft®, Ultra-Loft®, and Cotton Classic Batting Soft 'n Crafty® and Pop-in-Pillow® pillow forms

Stearns & Foster Company
P.O. Box 15380
Cincinnati, OH 45215
Mountain Mist® Bleached Cotton Batting, Mountain Mist® Cotton Gold, Mountain Mist® Polyester Batting, and Mountain Mist® Fatt Batt., Mountain Mist® Pillowloft Pillow Forms

Fabrics

Concord Fabrics, Inc.
1411 Broadway
New York, NY 10018

Gutcheon Patchworks
Dept. 8
611 Broadway
New York, NY 10012

Peter Pan Fabrics
Henry Glass & Company
1071 Sixth Avenue
New York, NY 10018

Graph Paper

BLD Enterprises
Betty L. Donahue
2624 West 155th Street
Gardena, CA 90249

(213) 324-2446

BLD can supply grid sheets heavy enough to hold the shape of your pattern pieces yet light enough to sew through easily. Ask for 4-to-the-inch grid sheets printed on index stock. Available by the sheet in 11" x 17", 9" x 12", and 8½" x 11" sheets. BLD has an impressive line of graph paper and grids suitable for all kinds of crafts projects.

Index